Third Edition

Data-Based Decision Making

EDIE L. HOLCOMB

A Joint Publication

Solution Tree

555 North Morton Street
Bloomington, IN 47404
800.733.6786 (toll free) / 812.336.7700
FAX: 812.336.7790

email: info@solution-tree.com
solution-tree.com

Printed in the United States of America

16 15 14 13 12   1 2 3 4 5

Library of Congress Cataloging-in-Publication Data

Holcomb, Edie L.
  Data-based decision making / Edie L. Holcomb. -- 3rd ed.
    p. cm. -- (Essentials for principals)
  Includes bibliographical references and index.
  ISBN 978-1-935543-02-2 (perfect bound) -- ISBN 978-1-935543-03-9 (library edition) 1. Educational evaluation--United States--Data processing. 2. School improvement programs--United States--Data processing. 3. Educational indicators--United States. I. Title.
  LB2822.75.H586 2012
  371.2'07--dc23
                        2011046198

Solution Tree
Jeffrey C. Jones, CEO
Edmund M. Ackerman, President

Solution Tree Press
President: Douglas M. Rife
Publisher: Robert D. Clouse
Vice President of Production: Gretchen Knapp
Managing Production Editor: Caroline Wise
Senior Production Editor: Suzanne Kraszewski
Copy Editor: Rachel Rosolina
Text Designer: Rian Anderson
Cover Designer: Amy Shock

ACKNOWLEDGMENTS

As in all things, I must first acknowledge and thank my husband, Lee Olsen, for his encouragement and support. The nutritious breakfasts he cooked for me after my early morning hours of writing spoke volumes for this man of few words.

I am thankful to Douglas Rife for approaching me about this volume in the *Essentials for Principals* series. His guidance and suggestions for revision clarified my thinking and strengthened the result, and I am honored to be among the authors engaged in this project. I also thank Solution Tree's entire editorial team for their assistance, suggestions, and support—especially Gretchen Knapp and Sue Kraszewski.

The administrators and teacher leaders who work in the trenches every day are my heroes. I wish I could name all those whose paths I've crossed. Some who provided specific insights and examples for this book include:

- Jane Chadsey and Laurie Wasson of the Renton, Washington, school district

- Steve Clarke of the Bellingham, Washington, school district

- Geri Santarelli of the Kenosha, Wisconsin, school district

- Roberta Selleck and her leadership team in the Adams 50 school district of Westminster, Colorado

- Gordon Oliver and the staff of Rockwood Elementary in Oklahoma City, Oklahoma

- Eva Kubinski of the special education team of the Wisconsin Department of Public Instruction

I am indebted to many and wish all a delightful and determined data journey!

* * *

Solution Tree Press would like to thank the following reviewers:

Wendy Birhanzel
Principal
Wildflower Elementary School
Colorado Springs, Colorado

S. David Brazer
Associate Professor, Department of Educational Leadership
George Mason University
Fairfax, Virginia

Jane N. Costa
Principal
Oak Street Elementary School
Basking Ridge, New Jersey

Ann Curry
Principal
Avondale Elementary School
Birmingham, Alabama

Karen Daugherty
Principal
Rose Tree Elementary School
Media, Pennsylvania

Bradley Geise
Data Services
Education for the Future
Chico, California

Walter Gordon
Principal
Cartersville Primary School
Cartersville, Georgia

Trent Kaufman
President and CEO
Education Direction
Salt Lake City, Utah

Mark Keen
Superintendent
Westfield Washington Schools
Westfield, Indiana

Laurie Pitre
Principal
North Bay Elementary
Biloxi, Mississippi

Kevin Schlomer
Elementary Literacy and Math Coach
Indianola Community School District
Indianola, Iowa

Jody Skidmore Sherriff
Regional Director, K–12 Alliance
WestEd
Santa Ana, California

Vanessa Stuart
Assistant Principal
Birmingham Elementary
Wylie, Texas

Cindy Wrenn
Principal
Signal Hill Elementary School
Manassas, Virginia

TABLE OF CONTENTS

Reproducible pages are in italics.
Visit **go.solution-tree.com/schoolimprovement** to download the reproducibles in this book.

ABOUT THE AUTHOR

Edie L. Holcomb, PhD, has been a principal, district administrator, and university professor and is highly regarded for her ability to link research and practice on issues related to school leadership, improvement, and reform. Her classroom experience includes teaching heterogeneous classes at all grade levels, inclusion of students with multiple disabilities, and coordination of services for gifted and talented students. Her building-level administrative experience ranges from affluent suburban schools to Title I schools with racial and ethnic diversity and English learners (ELs).

At the university level, Dr. Holcomb served as associate director of the National Center for Effective Schools, developing School-Based Instructional Leadership, a training program for site-based teams. As an associate professor of educational administration at Wichita State University in Kansas, she coordinated the principalship course and internships and taught applied inquiry in the field-based doctoral program.

Dr. Holcomb understands the challenges of districts with enrollment ranging from 3,000 to 45,000, having served as director of standards and assessment and later as supervisor of twenty-one schools in the Seattle School District in Washington. She also served as executive director of curriculum and instructional services in Kenosha, Wisconsin.

She has provided technical assistance for implementation of school improvement efforts throughout the United States as well as in Canada, Guam, St. Lucia, Hong Kong, and the Philippines. She helped develop Washington State's *School System Improvement Resource Guide* and worked with the Ohio Department of Education on its plans for technical assistance and support for districts and schools identified for improvement under No Child Left Behind. She has also worked with statewide models in Kentucky and Pennsylvania.

Dr. Holcomb holds a BS in elementary education, an MS in gifted education, and an EdS in educational administration. She received a PhD in educational administration from the University of Minnesota.

To learn more about Edie, visit her on the web at www.edieholcomb.org.

To book Edie for professional development, contact pd@solution-tree.com.

INTRODUCTION

In a recent data workshop, I asked participants to describe their feelings about data use in thirty seconds or less. One group penned the following paraphrase of a famous poem to express its sentiments about having plenty of data, but no opportunity to understand and use it:

> Data, data, everywhere—in every color ink!
>
> Data, data, everywhere—no time to stop and think!

Data-Based Decision Making is designed to help principals become more knowledgeable about how to use data themselves and support the use of data as one of their leadership responsibilities. Teaching and learning occur in the context of community values and in environments created at the school and classroom levels. This book shows principals a broader scope of data use with which they can lead staff to "become more proactive and move beyond the 'on the surface' work with data—and investigate 'below the surface' issues related to our data" (Creighton, 2007, pp. 1–2).

This book addresses three basic questions regarding data use:

- **What data are you looking for?** This question emphasizes data related to student learning, nonacademic student realities, staff-related information to guide supervision and support, and family or community factors. These data come from multiple sources and multiple years.

- **How will you find the data?** Reports of state assessments come automatically to the attention of school leaders but not necessarily in formats most useful to teachers for planning purposes. Other sources of data may be available, but school leaders do not currently access them for regular discussion. The need for other kinds of data surface as staff members assemble evidence to challenge their assumptions and to demonstrate the efficacy of their decisions. Some of these data are available or can be created at the school site. For other needs, the principal's connections to district staff are critical to facilitate necessary assistance.

- **How will you use the data?** Each chapter focuses on a specific purpose for data use, as outlined in the chapter overviews that follow. Many of the types of data recommended for use have multiple purposes and may be mentioned in more than one chapter. The application of the data is guided by protocols or questions that the principal may use to stimulate data discussions within the school.

Chapter 1 focuses on current best practices with data use, especially those associated with higher achievement in elementary schools. It also delineates the unique role of the principal and the influence she or he provides on the district, school, classrooms, and teachers.

Chapter 2 describes elements of the school culture and structure that must be considered and strengthened to create a data-friendly context for the work described in the remaining chapters. The previous edition of this *Essentials for Principals* volume described such factors as preconditions. This edition holds that issues of values, culture, and teamwork within the school are matters for ongoing attention, and that data can actually be used to help *build* those conditions. The principal should not delay use of data solely on the basis of the context not being ideal but should instead diagnose where steps need to be taken to facilitate the data work. This chapter stresses use of a broad range of data sources to increase the ability to make stronger decisions about both student learning and the environment. It also discusses the three questions of what data to look for, how to find it, and how to use it.

Chapter 3 focuses on data use for schoolwide decision making, a cyclical process that is briefly introduced in chapter 2. This chapter also addresses the three foundational questions about data use within the context of six components of school improvement.

Chapter 4 zeroes in on the use of data to identify and support struggling students. It also emphasizes the need to focus on the most essential concepts and skills (MECS) and clarifies the importance of formative assessment and changes in teacher record keeping. These data uses are linked to implementation of differentiated instruction and organized interventions. Student engagement with evidence of their own learning also depends on authentic, real-time assessment.

Chapter 5 addresses uses of data to strengthen classroom instruction. This chapter describes the intersection of evidence of implementation (from chapter 3) with the principal's role in teacher evaluation, supervision, and professional development. Once again, the text reinforces the necessity of developing assessment practices that provide usable, credible data.

Finally, chapter 6 focuses on the principal's own use of data for professional growth. It synthesizes the principal's responsibilities from earlier chapters in rubric form as a self-assessment tool. This chapter also provides examples of principals' goals related to data use, school improvement, and other aspects of leadership practice.

The three basic questions of data use (what kind, how to find, and how to use) are common elements throughout this book. Each chapter also closes with a section on your role as principal as it relates to data-based decision making. These sections include prompts for you to journal to record the observations, insights, and needs that surface. *The book will be of most value if you take this step seriously, because your journaling becomes anecdotal data that will shape your goals and next steps.*

The same group of workshop participants who expressed their sentiments about having plenty of data, but no opportunity to understand and use it, had a different outlook at the end of our workshop together. They shared their new learning about data use in a cheer, complete with makeshift pom-poms and not-so-agile leg kicks:

Give me a D!	**D!**
Give me an A!	**A!**
Give me a T!	**T!**
Give me an A!	**A!**
What does it spell?	**DATA!**
What is it FOR?	**STUDENT LEARNING!**

This book, written specifically for elementary principals, will help practitioners move their schools toward more and more intentional data use, which, in turn, will support greater student success.

1

Data, Decisions, and the Principal in the Middle

Data-based decision making is an essential part of principalship. The phrase "data for decision making" has been used so often in discussions of school improvement efforts that it has nearly become a meaningless mantra. The good news is that people no longer argue about whether you should use data. Effective use of data has been repeatedly tied to successful efforts to increase levels of student achievement. More data are available to support principals' and teachers' efforts to improve student achievement, and educators have become more sophisticated in their use of data. The increased emphasis on data use has prompted more training and heightened educators' awareness of how data can be used to help diagnose problems and identify possible solutions. Many schools have experienced an increase in the use of data, the types of data used, and the number of ways in which data are used.

The bad news is that schools sometimes use the wrong data in the wrong ways while neglecting other vital and useful information. The danger is a tendency to generate data for the sake of having more data, without creating the context in which those data will become useful information.

The No Child Left Behind (NCLB) goal was and is correct and critical: its public focus on equity has provided visibility and a forum for advocacy groups such as the National Association for the Advancement of Colored People, the National Council of La Raza, the Citizens' Commission on Civil Rights, and the National Center for Learning Disabilities (Shirley, 2009). In many schools and districts, the use of disaggregated data on state assessments has raised awareness of previously hidden or ignored achievement gaps. Though much remains to be done to close those gaps (Barr & Parrett, 2007), their reality is now abundantly clear.

The public visibility of state assessment systems and results has begun to build a sense of collective responsibility in another way. When state-mandated tests were given only in reading and math and at only one grade at each level—elementary, middle, and high—those test results were often given only to the teachers of the tested subjects or grades. Now, with the entire school judged as having made adequate yearly progress (AYP) or not and with data provided for more students, additional staff members participate in data discussions.

Developing a student-focused school culture calls for the use of data in conjunction with a stated mission. Such a culture necessitates an active dialogue among professionals about the moral purpose at the heart of the endeavor. Authentic involvement in articulating our shared beliefs represents one part of the picture. It must be accompanied by courageous identification and analysis of data aligned with each lofty phrase to determine whether an organization actually walks its talk. The pressures on schools since enactment of NCLB and the implication that the sole mission of a school is to ensure reading and math proficiency have overshadowed more general discussions of beliefs and values. As many educators have said, "Since NCLB, we don't have to bother with a mission statement any more. We just have to meet AYP."

In much the same way, assessment and accountability reports have focused the school's entire attention on the fundamental skills of reading and math. No one argues that these subject areas are crucial building blocks for present and future learning, but this narrow focus has led to school improvement plans that target only reading and math and ignore all other factors known to make a school a better, more effective learning organization.

Knapp, Swinnerton, Copland, and Monpas-Huber (2006) discuss this evolution in the use of data:

> An argument can be made that educational leaders have always had "data" of some kind available to them when making decisions intended to improve teaching and learning. Effective leaders gathered whatever information they could readily access, and then drawing on accumulated experience, intuition, and political acumen, they chose the wisest course of action to pursue. The data they collected was likely impressionistic and rarely systematic, complete, or sufficiently nuanced to carry the weight of important decisions. (p. 2)

Chapter 2 will outline a weighty set of data, and chapter 3 will describe a systematic process for effective uses of data in decision-making.

Effective Uses of Data

A review of literature on data use through the mid-2000s yielded twenty practices that were prevalent among schools and districts with consistent high achievement or significant gains (Holcomb, 2004). These high-performing organizations were characterized by:

1. Creating a culture of collective responsibility for all students

2. Understanding that assessment is an integral part of the instructional process

3. Testing their results against their espoused mission

4. Using data to stimulate equity conversations

5. Making clear distinctions between inputs (by adults) and outcomes (for students)

6. Using both objective and subjective (perceptual) data appropriately

7. Providing user-friendly data visuals

8. Focusing on the most critical priorities to conserve time, energy, and money

9. Drilling down for student- and skill-specific data in priority areas

10. Planning forward as students rise to the next grade or school, to respond to individual skill gaps

11. Planning backward to fill gaps revealed in the instructional program

12. Examining research, best practices, and exemplary schools

13. Reflecting on their practice by analyzing curriculum and instructional strategies

14. Selecting proven strategies for implementation

15. Identifying and planning for student populations with specific needs

16. Providing or developing formative assessments to balance large-scale, high-stakes tests

17. Monitoring rates of progress over time for both individual students and cohort groups

18. Gathering evidence about implementation of improvement strategies and their impact on student learning

19. Consolidating multiple plans

20. Taking the initiative to generate their own data and tell their own story, rather than relying on state reports and media coverage

Reports on data use have continued to underscore the value of utilizing data for the purposes of school culture building and decision making. A six-year study sponsored by the Wallace Foundation adds perspectives from the late 2000s. A seventeen-page section of Louis, Leithwood, Wahlstrom, and Anderson's (2010) report *Learning From Leadership* focuses specifically on "data use in schools and districts." After examining test data, conducting classroom observations, and gathering perceptual data from a wide range of respondents in 9 states, 43 school districts, and 180 elementary, middle, and high schools, Louis et al. (2010) write that "most principals have and use considerable amounts of evidence about the status of individual students and their student populations," but "very few principals have systematically collected evidence about the school and classroom conditions that would need to change for achievement to improve" (p. 179).

Types of Data Used by Principals and Teachers

All but one principal in the *Learning From Leadership* study referred to state-mandated assessment results when identifying the types of data used in their schools. Sixteen of the twenty-seven principals also referred to district-mandated measures of student achievement. A few talked about development of diagnostic and formative assessments used by teachers to track student performance and to provide targeted interventions. High data-use schools particularly emphasized development and systematic use of diagnostic and formative assessments of student learning.

The principals in the study also referred to evidence about their students as a group, including mobility rates, attendance, graduation rates, eligibility for free or reduced-price lunch, and students with various disabilities. At a minimum, they used these data to comply with policy requirements for reporting student test results and for allocating student and district resources. Less frequently, school and district personnel used student background information for help in interpreting student and school performance data. This complex use of data was more likely in high data-use schools.

High Data-Use Schools

One central finding of the *Learning From Leadership* study was that "high and low data-use schools differed little in respect to the data available to them. Differences were more evident in the *uses* schools made of the available data" (Louis et al., 2010, p. 191, italics added). Data uses more typical of high data-use schools than of low data-use schools include:

- Using data to monitor the outcomes of school improvement plans

- Using formative assessments of student progress at regular intervals throughout the year

- Using data in making decisions about professional development plans

- Using data in conversations with parents about student performance and programming

- Using data to move beyond problem identification to problem solving; gathering additional data to better understand the causes or factors related to the problems in question

Differences in data use between elementary and secondary schools were even more marked and paralleled the differences between high and low data use. When all schools were considered together, "the typical approaches to data use by districts and principals had no measurable influence on student learning. . . . *In elementary schools, however, data use may account for a significant proportion of the variation in student achievement, over and above the effects of student diversity, poverty and school size*" (p. 196, italics added).

The Position of the Principal

Figure 1.1 illustrates the unique position of the principal, her spheres of influence at the individual school site, and her connections with the district. All of the relationships shown here represent venues in which the principal must make and communicate decisions. These decisions can be better reached, explained, and evaluated using data.

The Principal at the Site

At the building level (right side of fig. 1.1), the principal works with many constituents outside the school through formal structures and individual interactions. Organizations like the parent teacher association (PTA) or a school council often represent families and community members. In addition, the principal meets with individual parents and needs to be aware of informal clusters (such as native-language groups) within the school attendance area.

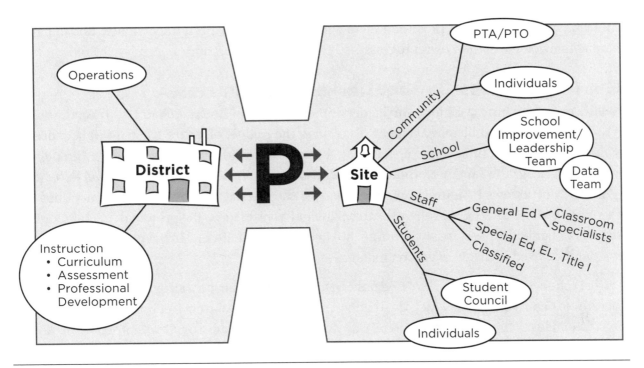

Figure 1.1: The position of the principal.

At the school site, the principal is more directly in charge of the formal structures for school-wide decision making. Such structures include a school improvement/leadership team (SI/LT) that addresses problem solving and planning around issues broader than individual classrooms. In all but the smallest elementary schools, the SI/LT should be supported by a data team with the more specific charge of gathering and displaying data needed for use at the school and classroom levels. These structures are further described in chapter 2.

The principal's most numerous and frequent interactions are with staff who work in the school. Figure 1.1 is far from complete, allowing space for just three of the many types of staff who support students in a variety of ways. One group of certificated (licensed) staff members consists of general education teachers who have their own classrooms or who serve all students in art, music, physical education, library, media, and so on. A second group of certificated staff includes teachers with specialized expertise to match specific student needs, such as special education and English learners (ELs). Classified (that is, noncertificated) staff provide a broad range of services for students, such as clerical, nutritional, custodial, and instructional. Pause in your reading and take time to personalize figure 1.1 so that it represents how the staff at your school would describe their groups. (See the reproducible template Position of the Principal on page 12.) Each group must be represented on the school improvement/leadership team. In addition, the principal should discuss data with small groups and individuals within the school as part of the ongoing supervisory relationship.

The fourth constituency represented in figure 1.1 is the student body. Some elementary schools have a formal student council structure, particularly for upper grades. The principal also interacts with all students informally in common spaces, with individuals in both commendation and consequence modes, and in the process of visiting classrooms. The role of data use with students includes gathering their perceptions, providing them with timely and meaningful feedback, and engaging them with evidence of their own progress.

The Principal as Connection to the District

Many principalship books focus on leadership at the school site and do not address the reality of the principal as middle management. The *P* is in the middle of figure 1.1 (page 9) because the principal must accept full ownership for what occurs at the school while operating within policies, procedures, programs, and performance expectations established at the district level (left side of figure 1.1). The arrows in figure 1.1 do not flow *from* the district to the principal; rather, they represent the district as another sphere for the principal *to* influence. The principal, in collaboration with his or her colleagues, must communicate needs, participate in district committees, and ask how data are used in district decision making.

Large school districts often have two organizational divisions: operations and instruction. The operations departments may include finance, legal, human resources, technology, and often the superintendent's office. The instructional side deals with curriculum, instruction, assessment, and professional development. Pause at this time and consider your direct supervisor's location within the organizational structure of the district. If, as principal, you report to operations, it is even more critical that you take the initiative and devote intentional time and energy to bridge and influence what occurs on the instructional side—for example, with regard to the *most essential concepts and skills (MECS)*, a term used frequently in this book. The prioritized learning targets, the MECS, cannot be chosen at will by individual teachers or schools, especially in systems where middle schools receive students from more than one site or where students are mobile within the district.

The types of data use described in this chapter may also generate the need for district help in accessing data sources and in providing technological support to set up record-keeping processes and to create user-friendly data displays. More sophisticated use of data at the school level must inform district decisions about data warehousing and will likely impact policies about grading and student placement. The data-skillful principal will be able to influence the district context on behalf of his or her school and students by asking questions about how data is used in district decisions and by presenting data that clearly describes the school's needs, decisions, and programs.

Your Role as Principal

Already in this chapter, the discussion of figure 1.1 prompted you to reflect on the constituents you serve at the school level, how they perceive their individual and group identities, and how they are represented in the formal decision-making structures in your school. Take time to journal your observations as part of your anecdotal data collection. You will further reflect on these observations as you read chapter 2 and when you complete the self-assessment in chapter 6.

The discussion of figure 1.1 also prompted you to think about your reporting relationship as well as involvement with district-level data use and decision making. Journal about your linkages to those structures. Unless you lead the only elementary school in the district, you also need to consider how you and your colleagues might share the load of being directly involved in district committees and how you share those experiences and gather reactions from each other. Some principals have—in good faith and because of the crushing load of work in limited time—entrusted the instructional work in their school to district curriculum consultants and district-based instructional coaches. These individuals have valuable expertise and connections to the classroom context, and they provide a valuable service. But you must not become disconnected from, or delegate to others, the instructional leadership role for your school.

Finally, you must assess your own assessment literacy. Michael Fullan (2003) describes assessment literacy as:

- Ability to gather dependable student data

- Capacity to examine student data and make sense of it

- Ability to make changes in teaching and schools derived from those data

- Commitment to communicate effectively and to engage in external assessment discussions

You need not have the statistical expertise of the data analysts in the state and district assessment departments, but you do need confidence and competence to hear and respond to teacher questions and concerns. You should also access your district connections to answer questions of a more technical nature.

The bottom line is this: it makes sense to use data to clarify decisions, identify alternative solutions to problems, and target resources more effectively. The real question is not *whether* to integrate the use of data into school leadership but *how*. At the same time, the reality is that identifying good data and using it effectively is a complex process—a challenge with which many schools still struggle. According to the Center for Comprehensive School Reform and Improvement (2006), "Data-driven decision making . . . reminds practitioners that their plans have a greater likelihood of succeeding if the goals and strategies within them are based on solid information and not on hunches or habit" (p. 1).

The purpose of this book is to help principals and schools grow beyond the proverbial description of being data rich and information poor—past being data-driven to perceiving their work as data-guided, or better yet, data-enriched. Almost anything you decide and do, you can decide and do better with skillful use of appropriate data.

Position of the Principal

Directions: Customize this figure using the groups and roles in your school and district. This figure can also be used in staff discussions that focus on how, when, where, and by whom data is used in your setting.

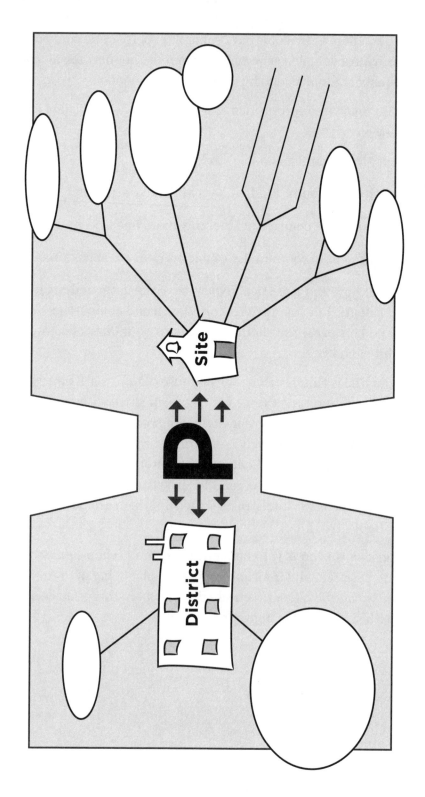

2

Creating the Context for Data Use

Chapter 1 introduced the concept of data-based decision making as an essential element of the principal's work along with the caution that introducing more data solely for the sake of being more data-based is misguided. Waiting until the conditions are optimum for data use, however, would also be an error. The principal's role is to work concurrently on cultural work and technical work, creating the context and motivation for data use as well as actually increasing the use of data. As Heritage and Yeagerly accurately assert, "For practitioners to develop a commitment to data use . . . school cultures that trust data and support high-quality data use must be nurtured" (2005, p. 334).

A data-friendly school culture might be described as a "culture of inquiry" (Earl & Katz, 2006). In such a setting, principals and other staff members develop an "inquiry habit of mind" that involves:

- Resisting the temptation to make decisions based on past practices

- Making a concerted effort to surface assumptions

- Challenging assumptions with objective evidence

- Having the courage to openly acknowledge that problems will always exist and should be raised and addressed

- Being confident that leaders and staff are capable of identifying and implementing solutions

Nurturing this inquiry habit of mind requires the principal to understand the power of organizational culture, diagnose the current culture and habits of mind, and cultivate improvement.

Cultivating the Culture

Fullan (2005) notes that "cultures consist of the shared values and beliefs in the organization" (p. 57). If those beliefs are not spelled out and used to ennoble efforts and to strive for a higher purpose, they remain at a level of nonchalant routine and slide away from true commitment during times of stress. School leaders must devote attention to cultivating the culture of the school even as it swirls around them. The end goal is to create a culture focused on the three commitments described by DuFour, DuFour, Eaker, and Karhanek (2010):

1. **A commitment to high levels of learning for all students.**

   The fundamental purpose of our school is to ensure all students learn at high levels, and the future success of students depends on how effective we are in achieving that fundamental purpose. There must be no ambiguity or hedging regarding our commitment to learning, and we align all practices, procedures, and policies in light of that fundamental purpose. We recognize that a commitment to the learning of each student means we must work together to clarify exactly what each student must learn, monitor each student's learning on a timely basis, provide systematic interventions that ensure a student receives additional time and support for learning when he or she struggles, and extend and enrich learning when a student has already mastered the intended outcomes. We also recognize that if all students are to learn at high levels, we must also be continually learning. Therefore, we must create structures to ensure all staff members engage in job-embedded learning as part of our routine work practices.

2. **A commitment to a collaborative culture.**

   We cannot achieve our fundamental purpose of learning for all if we work in isolation. Therefore, we must build a collaborative culture in which we work together interdependently and assume collective responsibility for the learning of all students.

3. **A commitment to using results to foster continuous improvement.**

   We will not know whether or not all students are learning unless we are hungry for evidence that students are acquiring the knowledge, skills, and dispositions most essential to their success. We must systematically monitor each student's learning on an ongoing basis and use evidence of that learning to respond immediately to students who experience difficulty, to inform our individual and collective professional practice, and to fuel continuous improvement. (p. 21)

Although the end goal is clear, how does a principal accomplish it? In the meta-analysis of principal leadership practices associated with student achievement conducted by Marzano, Waters, and McNulty (as cited in Reeves, 2007), only three of twenty-one leadership behaviors stimulated both the quick, easy changes and the more complex reforms that produced lasting systemic improvements. Those three behaviors were: (1) belief systems about the efficacy of leaders and teachers, (2) research-based practices, and (3) monitoring and evaluation. Since the early 1990s, school reform movements have focused attention on the last two leadership behaviors and ignored or even undermined the first.

Leaders must pay attention to the predispositions and reactions of staff when creating a sense of urgency and accountability. Conveying confidence in the ability and willingness of the staff, believing in them, and building their capacity are as critical as focusing their attention on the needs revealed in the data.

Leaders working to strengthen cultures should consider taking the following steps:

- Use a climate survey or externally facilitated focus groups to periodically and formally assess the culture.

- Use informal chats with both certificated and support staff to constantly assess the culture.

- Identify opinion leaders in various parts of the school, and connect with them regularly to glimpse what people are currently thinking and feeling.

- Use formal and informal assessment information to identify positive and negative factors and trends in the environment.

- Create space for people to vent their frustrations through brief, planned ice-breakers and openers, but keep them short. As one principal commented, "It's OK to vent your feelings. It's not OK to wallow around in them."

- Support the positive and work with the willing. Don't alienate those who are slow to believe, but don't obsess about them, either.

- Set new norms through group discussions (Holcomb, 2009), and then articulate and model those norms consistently. For example, be open and public about a new skill you are learning on the job yourself and reveal some of your own challenges.

- Follow up individually when norms are violated. Be gentle at first, but don't hesitate to defend and reinforce collaboratively developed norms.

- Develop new stories of success, renewal, and accomplishment from within the staff.

- Bring in new voices, and provide them with an audience.

- Identify teacher leaders as spokespersons for the initiatives that are under way.

- Provide praise and recognition, not because people are doing what *you* want, but because they are supporting the collective effort identified in *their* school improvement plan and individual goals.

Leaders should apply these strategies to all formal and informal interactions with every group of constituents.

Another role of the principal is to create or refine the structures and processes that will embed use of data into the events that occur in the daily life of the school.

Inclusive Structures for Data Work

Two structures that facilitate schoolwide use of data include the school improvement/leadership team and the more specialized data team (as shown in figure 1.1, page 9). These structures are considered *inclusive* because each staff member must understand how they are represented in decision-making processes and how they receive information about and provide input to planning that affects them. As Linda Lambert (2003) points out, "The benefits of participation—improved relationships, altered assumptions and beliefs, shared goals and purposes, increased maturity and cognitive complexity—emerge in a spiraling way: the greater the participation, the greater the development; the greater the development, the higher the quality of participation" (p. 12).

In their extensive study, Louis et al. (2010) also report effects of shared leadership and collective leadership on teachers and students. The term *shared leadership* denoted "teachers' influence over, and their participation in, schoolwide decisions with principals" (p. 41). *Collective leadership* referred to the broader participation of "organizational members and stakeholders" (p. 19). Key findings of the study include:

- Almost all people associated with high-performing schools have greater influence on school decisions than is the case with people in low-performing schools (p. 19).

- Higher-performing schools award greater influence to teacher teams, parents, and students, in particular (p. 19).

- School leaders have an impact on student achievement primarily through their influence on teachers' motivation and working conditions; their influence on teachers' knowledge and skills produces less impact (p. 19).

- When principals and teachers share leadership, teachers' working relationships are stronger and student achievement is higher (p. 37).

- Leadership effects on student achievement occur largely because effective leadership strengthens professional community—a special environment within which teachers work together to improve their practice and improve student learning. Professional community, in turn, provides a strong predictor of instructional practices that are strongly associated with student achievement (p. 37).

Consequently, the school improvement/leadership team and the data team are particularly important in the development of data use in the school.

The School Improvement/Leadership Team

The school improvement process should be open and participatory, involving teachers, administrators, support staff, students, parents, community representatives, and sometimes business partners in a variety of ways. Although students are the most intimately involved with teachers and are quite aware of their school's needs and successes, so far they have been the least integrated into analysis, decision making, and planning processes. Their participation in the formal leadership structure is important at the middle and high school levels but may be less appropriate in elementary schools. The decision to not include students is acceptable but should be made after discussion and not simply overlooked.

The school improvement/leadership team should include representation from every segment of school staff, as described in chapter 1. This team does not make decisions about how to improve the school in isolation. Rather, their discussions focus on how and when to engage others—peers, students, and constituents—in the decision-making processes. Team members prepare, plan, coordinate, orchestrate, and follow up on feedback from activities conducted with the full staff.

As described further in chapter 3, engagement of all staff is crucial at these decision points:

- Developing and affirming the school's mission

- Identifying significant, meaningful data to compile for the school portfolio

- Interpreting the data, requesting more data, and identifying areas of concern

- Focusing areas of concern to a few priorities, and developing goals

- Participating in study groups to further analyze data in priority areas and to recommend validated strategies

- Affirming the completed achievement improvement plan

- Participating in staff development to learn how to use new strategies and assessments

- Assessing progress based on evidence of implementation and evidence of impact on improved student learning

Lambert (2003) further describes the "high-leadership-capacity school" as follows:

> Teachers who exhibit vitality are energized by their own curiosities, their colleagues, and their students; they find joy and stimulation in the daily dilemmas of teaching and are intrigued by the challenge of improving adult learning communities. Teachers become fully alive when their schools and districts provide them with opportunities for skillful participation, inquiry, dialogue, and reflection. . . . Because teachers represent the largest and most constant group of professionals in schools and districts, their full participation in the work of leadership is necessary for high leadership capacity. (p. 32)

Inclusive structures for data use such as the school improvement/leadership team and data team will empower this important teacher leadership.

The Data Team

Although all categories of staff should be represented in the entire school improvement process and share in the decision making, teachers must be given special status in the actual gathering and analyses of data. Some will be unfamiliar and uncomfortable with this work. Leaders should be sensitive to these feelings and provide shelter for teachers—not to shield them from the realities in the data, but to provide them with a safe environment for exploration. All constituents have a right to data access, but teachers should have the first chance to examine and analyze data and to prepare to discuss the data with others. Boudett and Moody (2005) stress the importance of making data study a collaborative approach from the onset:

> Even in cases where one person is willing to assume primary responsibility for data work, it is important that that person not work alone. Assembling a group of people, assigning responsibility for specific tasks, and planning

how individuals will coordinate their efforts with each other and the rest of the school sends a message that using data in your school will be a collaborative effort. (p. 14)

Composition of the Data Team

The data team should be an extended subset of the school improvement/leadership team (SI/LT) to ensure that the two groups communicate closely and inform each other's work. The data team is a smaller group than the SI/LT and may not include a member from every grade or department. In fact, members of the data team may not be on the school improvement team but may possess the specific skills and interests needed for data work. For example, retired teachers volunteer to help in this endeavor at some schools.

Although constituents do not have a major hands-on role doing data work and developing the school improvement plan, they do need to be regularly informed and given the opportunity to provide their input and reaction to the decisions made at each critical step. Representation of parents and community is more typical on the school improvement/leadership team than on the data team, due to the time and type of work and to the privacy issues around student information. However, broad involvement of stakeholders at the key decision points (described in chapter 3) is possible and valuable through the use of ad hoc groups to accomplish specific tasks. Unlike standing committees, which have a limited number of seats available and require a long-range commitment, a series of ad hoc groups, each with a specific task and defined time frame, can provide more opportunities and connections.

Characteristics of the Data Team

Members of the data team should be individuals who get excited about data (Holcomb, 2004) and are comfortable working with them. People who may not have time or interest in the full set of responsibilities of the school improvement/leadership team may be willing and able to help identify, prepare, and interpret data in preparation for consideration by the leadership team or for sharing with the whole staff.

Data team members should, of course, be assessment literate, with particular expertise in determining whether data are dependable, making sense of them, displaying them, and discussing them. Unlike the list of statistical terms, definitions, and formulas we once stored in short-term memory for a statistics course exam, *assessment literacy* is described by Michael Fullan (2003) as follows:

- Ability to gather dependable student data

- Ability to examine student data and to make sense of it

- Ability to make changes in teaching and learning derived from those data

- Ability to communicate effectively and to engage in external assessment discussions

These skills also enable data team members to help other staff members make sense of data and determine whether the data are dependable. A key skill in helping translate data in a way that is understandable and meaningful to others is the ability to convert columns and rows of numbers into line and bar graphs, stacked bar graphs, Pareto charts, and pie charts.

In addition to these technical skills, the members of the data team should have strong relationships with other staff members, the trust and respect of staff, and a reputation for being totally objective.

Roles and Responsibilities of the Data Team

As shown in figure 1.1 (page 9), the school improvement/leadership team and the data team work in tandem with each other. For example, the SI/LT identifies information needed for school decision making, and the data team determines whether it already exists and how to collect and compile it. The data team also supports teachers in using data to make decisions about their classes and individual students.

Specific tasks of the data team include:

- **Gathering existing data.** After a decade of standards and accountability, most schools have access to more data than they realize or may routinely use. In fact, a new challenge is sorting out which data are most informative for the issues being considered.

- **Previewing data for relevance and usefulness.** This valuable role involves reviewing existing data in terms of its relevance to emerging questions and pending decisions. A courageous school improvement/leadership team will also notice patterns and trends that *should* be rising to the awareness of the school and brings them to the fore.

- **Creating user-friendly data displays.** When it comes to working with data, the saying *A picture is worth a thousand words* could be paraphrased *A graphic is worth a thousand cells of numbers*. When the data team has identified facts or findings that are important for staff use, they must then display this information in graphs or charts that Schmoker describes as "simple data that even a child could construe" (2010, p. 51). An effective graph or chart tells a story at a glance, like the graphics often featured in *USA Today*. The purpose of these data displays is to help convey and ensure an objective, commonly held reality that either confirms or confronts the stories that have shaped school actions in the past.

- **Planning and facilitating data events and conversations.** Traditions and rituals surround certain times of the year in schools, and the annual release of state assessment data has become a significant event. It is certainly a time for all staff to be updated on the results. However, the true goal of the data team is to create and support an environment in which data use is an assumed aspect of ongoing conversations and collaboration. In that capacity, the data team helps teachers tease out the data related to their own students and practices.

- **Summarizing significant trends and findings for dissemination and future reference.** Rather than try to challenge, explain, or defend data that are reported in the media, being proactive and creating short, effective descriptions of results achieved by the school is a better expenditure of energy. Even factoids of interesting information (for example, "Did you know that nineteen different languages are spoken by our students?") generate a better understanding of the school's challenges and accomplishments.

- **Leading the search for better data and data management.** As schools become more data-oriented, they identify needs for better assessments and look for better ways to keep records of student progress. They may also engage in action research that entails use of data to make comparisons before and after or between groups and classrooms. The data team should initiate, guide, and support such efforts.

Team Time

Schools have commonly held school improvement/leadership team meetings on a monthly basis and interspersed monthly data team meetings between SI/LT meetings in order to prepare data for use in schoolwide events, such as faculty meetings and designated professional development times. Three trends have increased the need for time for data work:

1. Expanded emphasis on use of data for both schoolwide and instructional planning

2. Greater numbers of data reports to be utilized

3. Emergence of data use in teacher collaboration, such as professional learning communities and grade-level or content-area teacher teams

The first steps in finding time for data work are to use electronic communication to minimize the time spent handling announcements and housekeeping items and thus consecrate the times when teachers can be together to do collaborative work on improving teacher practices and student learning. Often schools provide substitute teachers so the data team can meet during school hours. In some cases, the scarcity of substitute teachers—or the awareness that student learning is negatively impacted when the "real" teacher is away—has led to a different format in which school improvement/leadership teams and data teams meet for two to three hours outside the school day and are compensated accordingly.

Designated member(s) of the data team may need additional time for hands-on tasks such as preparing data displays. In some schools, relieving this key individual of supervisory duties (lunchroom, recess, and so on) affords the additional time needed to complete data-related tasks. The collective bargaining agreement in some districts provides for a stated number of hours for individually directed professional development. Data work and support of colleagues definitely qualifies as professional learning, making it possible for team members to essentially pay themselves by applying their data-work hours toward that contract provision.

Opportunities for Teacher Collaboration

As noted previously, one role of the data team is to support teachers in their use of data for instructional planning. A key component of effective systems is providing time for teachers to discuss the data and to work together to develop solutions. Teachers view this time as an opportunity both to develop their skills in data analysis and to brainstorm and share effective instructional strategies. These experiences build the "trust in fellow group members [that] allows you to bring a struggling student's work to the group without fear of being judged or criticized" (Langer, Colton, & Goff, 2003, p. 46). However, providing common planning time often proves to be difficult.

Cromey and Hanson (2000) describe systems used for scheduling teacher collaborations in four types of schools. These are described in figure 2.1 (page 22).

Training for Staff

Clearly, teachers and other staff members will need support and training in learning how to utilize data for a variety of important functions. Opportunities to learn how to analyze assessment data have typically been provided in a variety of ways, including:

- Staff development focused on how to interpret and analyze reports of assessment results

- Presentations by central office staff or principals to school staff, followed by a discussion of possible next steps

- One-on-one sessions of a principal, assistant principal, or lead teacher with a classroom teacher to review and discuss results from his or her classes and students

- Training of an in-school data expert, typically a teacher, who works with grade-level or subject-area teams to analyze data

The ability, capacity, and commitment to use data cannot be developed solely through traditional forms of training, such as courses and workshops, however. Developing this collective capacity is far more complex than acquiring individual knowledge and skill, and requires embedding data activities in the ongoing work of groups of professionals.

Finally, staff training should include encouraging teachers and other school staff to recognize the data analysis skills they already have. Earl and Katz (2006) refer directly to educators who feel they "cannot do this 'data stuff' because they are no good with math" when stressing that "data literacy is not the same as 'crunching numbers'" (p. 45). Earl and Katz describe *data literacy* as a thinking process that includes "standing back and deciding what you need to know and why; collecting or locating the necessary data; finding ways to link key data sources, ensuring that the data are worth considering; being aware of their limitations; thinking about what the results mean, and finally, systematically considering an issue from a range of perspectives so that you really feel that you have evidence to explain, support, and also challenge your point of view" (p. 45). These mindsets describe the culture of inquiry that the principal must nurture in the school.

Finally, increased data literacy often provides dual benefits, enhancing both school culture and data use. As teachers learn to use data, it not only becomes second nature, it also begins to affect other aspects of their teaching in a positive way. As Wade (2001) notes, "In learning to incorporate data analysis as a regular part of their professional activity, teachers become more reflective about their teaching practices, less reactive, less willing to accept easy answers, and more open-minded to solutions based on the data they gather" (p. 2).

	School A	School B	School C	School D
Time and Planning Strategies	Once a month, the school day begins two hours later; teachers meet during this time to engage in the activities described as follows. School makes up this accumulated time by extending the school year.	Once a week, school staff are released from school at least forty-five minutes early. This time is added to other days throughout the week. Once per week, the entire staff meets for one hour before school. Staff decrease the nuts and bolts of the meetings and prioritize work related to assessment.	Several days a year, teachers are released from duties and replaced by substitute teachers. Up to three times a year, teachers meet with the principal.	After school and periodically during school hours, teachers meet with each other. Teachers request time to meet during school hours, and substitutes are hired to support this. Once a week during their planning hours, teachers meet with grade-level and subject-area teams.
Activities	Staff rewrite district standards and realign the assessments they use accordingly. Staff continuously re-evaluate this work and discuss and plan changes as needed.	Staff use allotted time to align curriculum across grades and with state standards. This process is driven by student-assessment data. Staff continuously re-evaluate this work and discuss and plan changes as needed.	Staff discuss students' progress according to the developmental continuums written by school staff. Teachers administer individual assessments to students. Staff discuss reports on assessment data from the district research department.	Staff share knowledge gained from professional development activities that address curriculum and assessment. Staff also discuss student mastery of standards and other outcomes and intervention strategies.

Source: Cromey and Hanson (2000).

Figure 2.1: Scheduling approaches for teacher collaboration.

Just "doing data," however, does not make the effort worthwhile. Using the data in an understood process to make meaningful decisions is critical.

The Cyclical Process of School Improvement

The ultimate goal is to embed data use in the day-to-day operations of the school and as part of a continuous cycle of school improvement. As Depka (2006) points out:

> For data analysis to ultimately have an impact on student achievement, it needs to be part of a cyclical process. When data analysis is viewed as one step in a system, its use will become integral to the workings of an organization. Without a process, data analysis can be only an event. Time is spent viewing and analyzing data, but there is no intended result other than to comment on what is observed. Although time is not wasted, data viewed without a process will not likely become a catalyst for change. (p. 2)

The first role of the principal and the data team is to assemble the existing data into an organized collection that can be accessed electronically or in hard copy. Although electronic technology supports more comprehensive data collection and is consistent with environmental concerns, a *limited* number of paper data collections in the traditional three-ring binder format encourages more curious and casual data exploration by a broader range of individuals.

The cyclical process of school improvement used as a framework in this book includes six components of data use:

1. Assembling the data

2. Analyzing the current state

3. Assessing current efforts

4. Determining next steps

5. Ensuring implementation

6. Documenting results

Each of the six components (discussed in depth in chapter 3) addresses the three key questions: (1) What data are you looking for? (2) How do you find it? (3) How do you use it?

What Data Are You Looking For?

Data on student learning are of paramount importance. The school's results on state assessments are a given in today's environment. Other kinds of data related to student learning are presented in figure 2.2 (page 24).

- State assessment data; multiple years
- Summaries of collaborative analysis of student work samples
- National norm-referenced tests—such as Iowa Tests of Basic Skills, California Achievement Test
- Criterion-referenced (standards-based) tests— such as state, local, National Assessment of Student Progress
- Ratings from team projects and exhibitions
- Curriculum-based classroom assessments
- Districtwide benchmark assessments
- Common formative assessments
- Beginning- and end-of-year tests
- Local unit tests
- Grades as reported to parents
- Performance checklists

Figure 2.2: Student learning data.

Data about student learning describe the current status of students but do little to illuminate possible causes or to inform appropriate strategies for addressing student needs. For those purposes, nonacademic student data are more useful. These types of data are outlined in figure 2.3.

- Student demographics
  › Gender
  › Racial/ethnic groups
  › Home language
  › Socioeconomic status
  › Mobility
- Disciplinary referrals and actions
  › Overall numbers of referrals and actions
  › Number of referrals and actions by subgroup
  › Proportion of referrals to actions
  › Ratio of referrals to actions by subgroup
- Observation logs
  › Staff
  › Students
- Checklists, rating scales
- Student survey data
- Attendance
  › Overall
  › By identifiable subgroups
  › Chronic absentees
- Homework completion rates
- Journal entries, anecdotes
  › Staff
  › Students
- Student focus group data

Figure 2.3: Nonacademic student data.

The increased rigor of student learning standards places increased demands for content knowledge on teachers, particularly at the elementary and middle school levels. For example, many experienced teachers began their careers when elementary mathematics focused primarily on computation and story problems. In past years, math content did not include statistics and probability, and teaching for conceptual understanding was emphasized less than providing practice in the algorithm that would yield the correct answer. This makes information about teacher preparation relevant and valuable to customizing teacher support. Consistent attendance by students is mirrored by the need for consistent and continuous instruction by teachers. For any number of legitimate and understandable reasons, teacher attendance can be a factor that needs to be explored in order to address student growth. Other kinds of staff-related data are presented in figure 2.4.

- Demographic distribution
  - › Gender
  - › Race/ethnicity
- Years of experience
- Areas of certification
- Professional development participation and specialties
- Perceptual data
  - › Surveys
  - › Focus groups

- Locations of experience
  - › Other schools
  - › Other districts
  - › Other states
- Years since completed undergrad
- Graduate degrees
- Days absent from classroom per year
  - › Health, unique family situations
  - › Professional involvement

Figure 2.4: Staff-related data.

A fourth category of important information includes data about families and communities within the service area of the school. All schools benefit from parent involvement and good communication with families, and Title I schools are specifically mandated to work directly with parents. Data on factors like those presented in figure 2.5 help determine methods of communication, involvement, and even locations for events like parent conferences and curriculum nights.

- Demographics
  - › Race/ethnicity
  - › Age
  - › Households with school-aged children
  - › Households with children at this school
- Attendance at parent-teacher conferences
- Perceptual data
  - › Interviews
  - › Focus groups
  - › Surveys

- Neighborhood concentrations
- Chamber of Commerce
- Census Bureau
- Realtors' association
- Participation as volunteers
- District transportation department

Figure 2.5: Sources of family and community data.

How Will You Find the Data?

The first message of caution and reassurance is this: you are unlikely to find all of the data listed in figures 2.2–2.5. If you do, you would be unwise to introduce all of it into a whole-faculty data event right off the bat. City, Kagle, and Teoh (2005) suggest that principals working to establish a more comprehensive approach to data use in their schools should first consider the following:

> How much time do you have to collect and analyze the data? What other resources do you have available to you? The answers to these questions influence how many data sources you can examine and which ones you choose. (p. 113)

Depka reinforces the need to "be selective about the data you choose" (2006, p. 22). She elaborates:

> The data you select should relate to your goal. If the plan is to analyze student achievement data, choose the sources that will give you the best all-around indications. It is important to provide enough data so that participants can have a good degree of confidence that their observations are accurate. Too much information at one data delve can overwhelm, confuse, and exhaust people. There is certainly a time and place to view it all, but the data should be viewed in segments to avoid data overload. (p. 22)

The principal and data team must consider the list of data as if it were a set of clues for a treasure hunt. Some of the data are directly at hand in the form of state and district reports. Other data (for example, work completion) are kept by teachers but may not have been collected in any systematic way or correlated with academic progress. Some data are compiled at the district level for reporting to the state but may not be broken down by school and shared with individual principals.

How Will You Use the Data?

Assembling the existing data involves searching for them, gathering them together, and previewing them in terms of how user-friendly they are and how well they connect to the perceived needs of the staff. For example, some data on student learning may be available but not easily used by teachers. In some states, it is difficult to access and aggregate specific information from individual student data because that information is included only in the individual reports that go directly to parents. In other cases, helpful data are provided only as spreadsheets of eye-numbing rows and columns that should be reformatted in the form of graphs before presentation.

In situations when new (previously unused) data are plentiful, the data should be made available to those who are immediately interested. But public display and large-scale dissemination and discussion of such new data should be reserved until it becomes meaningful for a question or issue raised throughout the school.

One way to think about prioritizing the display and dissemination of data is to ask, "What are the hot-button issues smoldering in 'lounge talk' in the school at this time?" Any data connected to current needs and interests can be raised to priority level for immediate use. As Boudett and Steele (2007) note, "researchers studying schools and other workplaces have found that leaders who are most successful at transforming their organizations are those who know how to frame important questions and then engage their colleagues in finding creative answers" (p. 2).

Another way to think about assembling existing data and prioritizing them for use is to consider the snowball approach to data leadership: provide enough data to generate discussion and to surface doubts and questions. Lead the data team in search of answers to the specific questions that arise and bring back that information, which adds to the data collection and may generate another set of questions. Thus the collection continues to grow, much as rolling a small snowball in snow eventually creates the bigger snowballs needed to create an all-out snow sculpture.

Once assembled and displayed, the data can be used to analyze the current state of student learning and school factors, to determine steps to be refined and new ones to be added, to guide implementation of new strategies and practices, and to verify that all the effort has made a difference.

Your Role as Principal

Challenging as it is, using data to improve teaching and learning is possible. Boudett and Steele (2007) indicate that "the key lies in building a school culture in which faculty members collaborate regularly and make instructional decisions based on evidence about students' skills and understanding" (p. 2). Principals who want to build a culture of data use in their schools must look first to themselves. Ask yourself, "Am I demonstrating use of data in making decisions—or do staff members only hear me talking about the importance of using them?"

The chicken-and-egg dilemma of which comes first—changed beliefs or changed behaviors—enters into discussions about commitment to use data and to accept responsibility for the results. Sometimes beliefs do not change until the professional behavior and actions of others actually *change the data* and prove what students can accomplish. While challenging beliefs, the leader must be willing to focus on behavior. Initially, staff members may not universally share a high regard and enthusiasm for working with data, but they must not be allowed to sabotage the effort with actions such as skipping meetings where data will be involved, undermining colleagues' efforts, and criticizing leaders' efforts in classrooms with students. Bryk and Schneider (2002) write about trust in schools and point out that unwillingness to confront inappropriate behavior sends the message to everyone in the organization that the behavior is acceptable and actually reduces the teachers' levels of trust in their principals.

Reporting on their *Learning from Leadership* study, Louis et al. (2010) emphasize that "leadership is second only to classroom instruction as an influence on student learning. After six additional years of research, we are even more confident about this claim. To date we have not found a single case of a school improving its student achievement record in the absence of talented leadership" (p. 9). The authors also report, "Where principals do not make data use a priority—where they do not mobilize expertise to support data use and create working conditions to facilitate data use in instructional decision making—teachers are not likely to do it on their own" (p. 179).

As principal, your role is critical. Take time to assess the culture of your school and to compare it with the characteristics of an inquiry-oriented culture. Consider the culture-shaping strategies in the early part of this chapter, and select some immediate next steps you can employ. Then reflect on the structures and processes that guide decision making in your school. Are they inclusive and intentional? Has adequate time and training been provided? Finally, review the types of data that are suggested and identify those now in use, those you believe can be added to current discussions, and those you can postpone for later in your school's efforts. The reproducible Is My School Culture Inquiry Oriented? (page 28) will guide you in this assessment.

Is My School Culture Inquiry Oriented?

How does the culture of my school compare with the characteristics of an inquiry-oriented culture?	
What strategies will I use to strengthen the culture for use of data?	
What existing structures and processes in my school involve and enhance use of data?	
How can I strengthen the use of data integrated in existing structures and processes? Do I need to add representation? Expectations? New processes?	
Of the student learning data sources (figure 2.2), which do we have and use? Have but not yet used? Need to access and use?	
Of the nonacademic student data sources (figure 2.3), which do we have and use? Have but not yet used? Need to access and use?	
Of the staff-related data sources (figure 2.4), which do we have and use? Have but not yet used? Need to access and use?	
Of the family and community data sources (figure 2.5), which do we have and use? Have but not yet used? Need to access and use?	

3

Data to Guide Schoolwide Decisions

In an effective educational system, data-based decision making occurs at many levels (Holcomb, 2012). Central office teams make decisions that impact all schools, but the principal's role and unique position in exerting influence on those decisions are vital. While chapters 4 and 5 describe decision making on a more individual basis—to support struggling students and to strengthen classroom instruction—this chapter deals with uses of data to address schoolwide issues, often as incorporated into school improvement plans. These decisions encompass, but are not limited to, academic needs. Student learning is affected by many conditions in the learning environment—from behavior expectations in common areas (such as hallways, lunchroom, playground) to unspoken expectations about student potential and to staff interactions with each other. As Killion and Bellamy (2000) remind us:

> Without analyzing and discussing data, schools are unlikely to identify and solve the problems that need attention, identify appropriate interventions to solve those problems, or know how they are progressing toward achievement of their goals. Data are the fuel of reform. . . . In short, using data separates good schools from mediocre schools. Schools that are increasing student achievement, staff productivity and collegiality, and customer satisfaction use data to inform and guide their decisions and actions. Data use essentially sets a course of action and keeps staff on that course to school improvement and student success.

That course of action consists of the following six components of data use, as introduced in chapter 2:

1. Assembling the data

2. Analyzing current status of student learning and school factors

3. Assessing current efforts

4. Determining next steps

5. Ensuring implementation

6. Documenting results

Some readers will recognize these components of data use as parallel to stages in a cycle of inquiry or action research. They are intentionally referred to as *components* of data use rather than as *steps* or *stages*. They do often occur in sequence (as would steps or stages), since they represent a logical flow from information to action to evaluation. In a true culture of inquiry, however, aspects of any or all of these components may occur at any time. Assembling the data collection, for example, is a continuous process as new data are generated or new questions are raised that tap into existing data in a new way.

This chapter explores how each of the six components of data address the three basic questions: (1) what data, (2) how will you find it, and (3) how will you use it? The closing section, "Your Role as Principal," summarizes these components.

Assembling the Data

As discussed in earlier chapters, creating the context for data use includes organizing or refining the structures and operations of the school leadership/improvement team and data team. Their roles include initiating a data collection to encompass four categories of data related to (1) student learning, (2) nonacademic student characteristics, (3) staff-related information, and (4) family and community factors. Sorting out what's available and used from what's available but not used, and prioritizing the introduction of previously unused data are part of their responsibility. This section looks more closely at two different kinds of data within each of the four categories listed in figures 2.2–2.5 (pages 24–25): *objective data* and *subjective* (or *perceptual*) *data*. Data from objective measures, such as standardized assessments, are sometimes referred to as *hard data*, while data based on human subjective perceptions of their experiences with the school or district are sometimes referred to as *soft data*. Common practice has included the use of objective data related to student learning, nonacademic student factors, and staff-related information, but has slighted the use of subjective data. Subjective data about students, families, and communities are not receiving adequate attention on a regular basis.

What Data Are You Looking For?

Prior to the demands of No Child Left Behind, school accreditation and school improvement models included a cycle of gathering input from stakeholders, typically through surveys. Now when schools are asked about stakeholder input, the answer too frequently is, "Well, yes, we used to give a survey to community, staff, and students so we could get their opinions and compare their perceptions, but we haven't done that in quite a while. We've had to really focus on just getting our state scores up." Both parents and nonparents have perceptions, concerns (accurate or not), and visions for their schools that are likely to be broader than "making AYP." Communicating with and engaging a community requires hearing from them and using that perceptual data as clues to find points of leverage that help move the school forward.

Incorporating data about and from families and communities is an ethical necessity. Fortunately, it also has documented benefits for the bottom line of improving student achievement. The *Learning from Leadership* study (Louis et al., 2010) documented implications for policy and practice related to parent and community engagement. They concluded,

> In their efforts to improve student achievement, school- and district-level leaders should, as a matter of policy and practice, extend significant decisional influence to others in the school community. Compared with lower achieving schools, higher-achieving schools provided all stakeholders with greater influence on decisions. The higher performance of these schools might be explained as a consequence of the greater access they have to collective knowledge and wisdom embedded within their communities. (p. 35)

In order to capitalize on this important knowledge and wisdom that resides in their communities, schools must intentionally create opportunities to gather perceptual data.

How Will You Find the Data?

Objective data are usually available in various reports and databases kept at the school or district level. Subjective data may also be available but not gathered in a systematic way for consideration as a whole school. For example, anecdotal notes kept by teachers might be considered subjective (versus quantified) data about student learning, and they may be used by many of the teachers but in a variety of formats. Teacher collaboration to create a common template would allow teachers to compare and discuss their observations.

Subjective data that capture the perceptions of staff, students, and parents more typically come from surveys or focus groups. The mechanism for gathering student perceptions can be modified to fit the ages of the students. Survey questions can be written in student-appropriate language, and primary students can respond by marking a range of facial expressions (for example, smiley faces, frowns, puzzled looks, and sad faces) when an adult reads the items. An elementary version of focus groups can be conducted during class meetings, when teachers agree to ask a few questions in all classrooms and make notes of the answers they hear. Teachers then provide their notes to the data team, which compiles these data and looks for common themes.

How Will You Use the Data?

The initial and ongoing purpose of the assembled data is for analyzing current problems and needs and assessing the effectiveness of plans and programs put in place to meet them. Objective data often reveal *what* the problems are and can be queried using the sets of guiding questions provided later in this chapter. Subjective data can also reveal needs and have the added value of providing clues about *why* certain situations may exist. In particular, perceptual data can help identify leverage points and suggest strategies that may impact those situations most directly.

A general protocol for discussion of survey data includes the following five steps, which may be performed in any sequence but should all be included in the process.

1. Identify the overall highs and lows for each group of respondents (such as teachers, administrators, students).

> › What were the highest three categories in terms of agreement within each group?

> › What were the lowest three categories in terms of agreement?

2. Compare your school's responses to any comparison groups, if they are provided (such as benchmark schools, district averages, state averages).

> › What were the top three categories of agreement in the comparison schools?

> › What were the lowest three categories in the comparison schools?

> › Which categories were rated similar to yours?

> › Which categories did your respondents rate differently from comparison schools?

> › Within the categories of disagreement, what were the specific items? Which of those specific items contributed to lower/higher responses?

3. Compare responses among groups within the school.

> › Which categories showed the highest agreement among groups of respondents (such as "teachers and administrators responded the same")?

> › Which categories represented the greatest discrepancy between groups?

> › Which specific items in those categories had disparate responses?

4. Identify the areas for celebration.

> › Which categories had the highest ratings by all groups?

> › Which categories had the highest levels of agreement?

> (Even when participants have a high level of agreement around a negative response, it is still good news. It means participants have the same perception, which provides a shared foundation for action.)

5. Identify areas of greatest concern or urgency for attention in planning.

> › Which categories had the lowest ratings?

> › Which categories had the greatest disagreement among groups?

These observations become part of the data set used in the next component, analyzing current status.

Analyzing Current Status

The data team compiles the data for review and reaction, but all staff members need to be involved in interpreting what the data mean and how the data should influence school decisions and improvement plans. Leaders must designate a time and develop a facilitated activity to engage staff in serious discussion to develop or affirm the school's mission as well as to interpret the data, request more information where needed, and identify areas of celebration and concern.

What Data Are You Looking For?

One approach to analyzing the current status of the school is to affirm the moral purpose and core values held by its members and to then determine whether and how well the school is adhering to that purpose and those values. This utilizes existing data but organizes them according to the key phrases of the school's mission statement. For example, if the mission statement includes "mastering academic skills," the objective data on student achievement are used to assess the level of progress toward that goal. If a belief in "developing good citizens" is expressed, then a discussion of the characteristics of a good citizen of the school community could align with data on attendance, behavior, and work completion.

Another approach to organizing the data in a meaningful way for analysis is to consider whether there are any hot-button issues being discussed among staff. Aligning data with questions of interest to staff creates more interest and motivation to engage in data discussions.

The end result of assembling the data and analyzing current status is a list of key findings under the headings of *strengths* and *needs*, which are sometimes perceived more positively with the terms *celebrations* and *concerns* (Holcomb, 2012).

How Will You Find the Data?

Most of the objective data needed to analyze current status are already available, although they may need to be formatted into more user-friendly data displays. Satisfaction or climate surveys may need to be administered to provide subjective data for your data collection.

How Will You Use the Data?

The following set of generic questions can apply to all types of data and be used as part of staff activities, such as small group exercises at tables or a data carousel (see Holcomb, 2004, for an explanation of this activity).

- **What do these data seem to tell us?** The word *seem* in this question acknowledges that staff will make inferences about information that is not used frequently in schools and is less familiar.

- **What do the data *not* tell us, and what *else* might we need to know?** This query prompts the need for deeper understanding and may identify follow-up steps for clarification.

- **What good news from these data can we celebrate?** The tendency to rush toward the negative is strong, and this question prompts attention to any good news that may be drawn from the data.

- **What needs for school improvement might arise from these data?** The word *might* reminds participants that these are tentative conclusions and ideas to be noted for further discussion as the school considers next steps.

The following questions serve particularly well as a protocol for discussing student-learning data:

- In which strands (for example, benchmarks or skills) are our students making the most progress? In which strands are they making some progress?

- In which strands do many students have ongoing challenges?

- Do all student groups show evidence of the progress we're making? If not, what are the differences?

- Do all student groups experience the same challenges? If not, describe the differences.

The resulting data summary of key findings will be used by the SI/LT to engage staff in assessing current efforts and determining next steps.

Assessing Current Efforts

The concept of using data analysis to identify school improvement steps does not imply that principals and schools are not already working to increase student achievement and aspects of the learning environment. School improvement truly is a *continuous* process, and periodic reviews of what's going on in the school can help focus efforts and conserve limited human and fiscal resources. This component and the use of data to ensure implementation and document results are similar to some aspects of program evaluation. (The *Essentials for Principals* series includes a volume, *Effective Program Evaluation,* specifically aimed at this.) The first step in analyzing current efforts is doing a *strategy search* to ensure that all the initiatives under way in the school are compiled into the big picture of change. Assessing current efforts leads to decisions about whether current initiatives should be continued, refined, or abandoned and replaced.

What Data Are You Looking For?

The component of data use to analyze current efforts should begin with questions like, What have we already been working on? and What strategies did we put in place to address our needs? Review of the data that led to those efforts leads to further examination, including the queries: What improvements did we see in the areas we've been working on? To what do we attribute those changes? How will we celebrate those successes and sustain those efforts?

How Will You Find the Data?

Most of the needed data will be part of the assembled data collection already in use. However, a unique aspect of this component of data use is its potential connection to grants and to district-initiated change mandates. If the new programs or practices are grant supported, the grant applications may include the data that supported the application and the data that must be provided for the grant evaluation. The principal and the data team need to make sure the required data are part of the available and usable information.

The summary of key findings under the headings of celebrations and concerns is valuable for this purpose. Evidence of success noted for celebration provides clues about what needs to be sustained. Schools (and principals) must not assume that gains will automatically continue without ongoing attention and support. Using data to identify concerns also helps identify current efforts that are not succeeding or areas of need that have not yet been addressed.

How Will You Use the Data?

The traditional five Ws and H from the field of journalism—what, who, when, where, why, and how—provide a set of guiding questions for discussion of data related to current efforts, particularly to change initiatives, as follows:

- What patterns do we see?

- Who are the students predominately represented in the patterns we see?

- When are those patterns more evident?

- Where do incidents most frequently take place?

- Why do we think these patterns have emerged?

- How should we confirm our interpretations? What actions might we take if we're right? Where else will we look if we're wrong?

Then the conversation can turn to consideration of whether and what new strategies should be added to our efforts. Key questions in making that determination include:

- What did we attempt that doesn't seem to have been effective yet?

- Do we have evidence that we fully implemented those changes?

- If our current strategies are not achieving their intended outcomes, what does the perceptual data indicate may be the matter? Are more training and support needed? Is there resistance to the initiative(s)? Of what nature? From what source? Are the strategies and the actual needs that have become clearer through analysis of the data mismatched?

The notes from these discussions help determine which current efforts should be sustained as next steps, which should be clarified and strengthened, which should be abandoned, and what needs are not currently being addressed.

Determining Next Steps

In many models of school improvement, the process of determining next steps based on data analysis would be described as the *plan stage*. It involves staff focusing the areas of concern, developing goals, and participating in study groups to seek validated strategies and recommend actions.

The adequate yearly progress benchmarks of No Child Left Behind influence goal-setting in the critical areas of reading and math. For other concerns being addressed with next steps, setting goals that match the SMART criteria of specific, measurable, attainable, results based, and time bound (O'Neill & Conzemius, 2006) is recommended. The school leadership/improvement team receives recommendations from study groups, synthesizes a draft set of action plans, and presents the plans to the full staff for affirmation.

What Data Are You Looking For?

Analysis of current status and assessment of current efforts generates a set of celebrations and concerns. You must resist the natural tendency to skip over the celebrations at this point. Many elementary schools have experienced the reality of working very hard on literacy and making gains in reading only to then turn their attention to math and see the gains in literacy and reading begin to slide. When data show high performance and/or significant progress, those data need to be discussed so the successful efforts can be intentionally included in the next steps moving forward.

In searching for next steps with a high probability of success, two other types of data work may be required. First, general data may identify a concern and suggest some possible solutions. In that case, more detailed analysis is needed to ensure the apparent solutions match the true (root) cause.

Second, as study teams investigate possible next steps, they should also conduct a data search—but this time for other people's data. Technology has made it easier to look for articles, attend webinars, and network with other educators. However, technology has also made it easier for marketing to masquerade as research. It is essential to look for reported data to support authors' and vendors' claims of being research based.

How Will You Find the Data?

The data analyzed to identify celebrations and concerns may need to be dissected further to ensure that the solutions being considered will directly match the real problems they are targeting. This deeper analysis is sometimes referred to as *drilling down* or *peeling back* the layers of data for more specific information. For example, perceptual data from staff at an elementary school clearly showed a major stress around students arriving in their classrooms to start the day "all riled up" and "already fighting." Teachers felt they were losing instructional time to get students calmed down and resolve conflicts. The principal had conducted his own analysis to determine *when* referrals came to the office and noted that a large proportion of the office referrals for discipline were occurring early in the day. Discussion turned from *when* the problem occurred to the data-backed reality that most of the students came to school on buses, which led staff to investigate ways to improve behavior management during the bus trips. They came back with recommendations that teacher aides be hired as bus monitors or that, as a less desirable but less expensive alternative, video monitors be installed on the buses.

Meanwhile, the data team and principal took another look at the specific behavior incidents and classified them as to *type*, creating a Pareto chart (Holcomb, 2009; Holcomb, 2012) that clearly showed that the largest portion of morning behavior incidents was related not to violation of bus rules but to violation of school rules. In actuality, students were getting "riled up" during the break-fast program and on the playground and *not* on the buses, which turned the process of determining next steps in a completely different direction.

This example illustrates how schools can make poor decisions even with data when they do not take time to engage in a *root-cause analysis* process. Displaying the data in a more meaningful way helped the group in this example to become clearer about the real causes needing to be addressed. An excellent tool for this purpose is the cause-and-effect (fishbone) diagram (see figure 3.1, page 38). Other tools for root-cause analysis include "Ask why five times," force-field analysis, and "Go for the green." (Facilitation tips for all of these are included in Holcomb, 2009.)

The fishbone diagram in figure 3.1 was created by a small group of workshop participants in a conference focused on increasing the success of special education students who were not eligible for the alternative state assessment and would have to take the regular state test. Various aspects of accommodations and interventions had already been explored, but uneasiness was building. In this case, the root-cause analysis process revealed the "elephant in the room," the obvious truth: the assessment was based on the standards covered in the general education curriculum. If these students were not exposed to the content being assessed, accommodations would not increase student success. The question for the root-cause analysis then became, What factors might contribute to lack of access to the general education curriculum? (Any issue can be analyzed with this tool if the stem question is completed with a relevant, specific noun phrase.)

The group's responses to the analysis question generated new factors: students missing regular class to attend a support program, teachers misusing/misunderstanding differentiation, escalating behavior, setting up "places to fix" students, and lack of time for collaboration between general and special education teachers. Each of these new factors was recorded on a bone of the fishbone diagram. As more ideas were generated, they became barbs attached to the appropriate bones. For example, group members realized that if students were pulled from a grade-level class for intervention time and the time was then used to remediate or reinforce lower-level skills, the students would not even be exposed to grade-level material they might process orally or visually, even if not through reading.

In some cases, this kind of root-cause analysis deepens and subdivides further, such as when, in this workshop, various perspectives on differentiation began to surface. One participant mentioned, "You can't differentiate on everything; you have to focus on the most essential learning outcomes." Others chimed in with comments such as, "We don't, because we think everything is essential," "There's no consistency in how we do differentiation," and "We don't know for sure what's most essential"—all of which denoted a deeper cause: the lack of shared professional development. As the discussion continued, new connections were made and dotted lines were added to show how lack of time for collaboration was linked to lack of shared ownership, lack of shared professional development, and lack of shared classroom rules and procedures. With this heightened awareness of the implications of lack of collaboration came renewed commitment to the next steps of collaborating with their building administrators to carve out opportunities to work together.

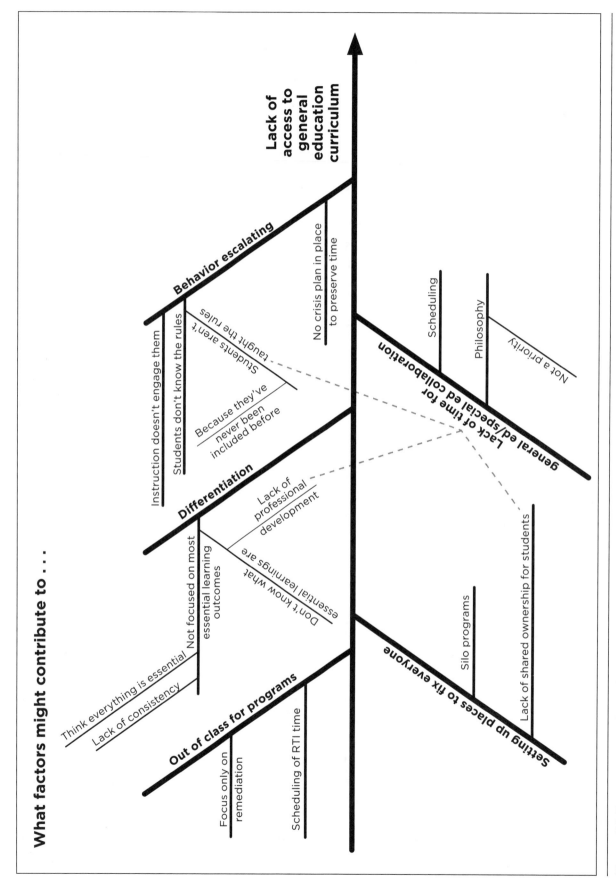

What factors might contribute to . . .

Lack of access to general education curriculum

Behavior escalating
- Instruction doesn't engage them
- Students don't know the rules
- Because they've never been included before
- No crisis plan in place to preserve time

Differentiation
- Think everything is essential
- Not focused on most essential learning outcomes
- Lack of consistency
- Don't know what essential learnings are
- Lack of professional development

Out of class for programs
- Focus only on remediation
- Scheduling of RTI time

Lack of time for general ed/special ed collaboration
- Scheduling
- Philosophy
- Not a priority

Setting up places to fix everyone
- Silo programs
- Lack of shared ownership for students

Figure 3.1: Root-cause analysis (fishbone) diagram.

How Will You Use the Data?

Based on a summary of the findings about current status, assessment of current efforts, and root-cause analysis, the school sets priorities for attention and researches effective practices that show evidence of matching those specific needs. The SI/LT compiles the recommended strategies and assesses them according to a specific set of questions. The group then presents the recommended strategies to staff for discussion of the same questions and validation of the next steps.

All staff members need the opportunity to engage in a holistic analysis of what they have planned. Before asking staff to affirm their commitment, these are the questions that must be addressed:

- Will the combined impact of this set of strategies raise achievement for all students?

- Will the combined set of strategies also directly address disparate learning needs and narrow achievement gaps?

- Have strategies been identified to resolve conditions in the learning environment and in the school culture that negatively impact student success and teacher practice?

- Will the combined set of strategies involve every adult in the school? Does every staff member see their contribution and the expectation it sets for them?

- Is the overall school improvement plan an ambitious stretch but manageable and necessary? What support will staff need?

All members of the school community must understand the big picture, know what's coming next and why, and have confidence that they will receive the support they need.

Ensuring Implementation

The strategies employed in school improvement represent *inputs* to the system made by the adults in the school. *Outcomes* are the actual results—hopefully, improved—that occur in student success (academic and nonacademic) related to those actions. The visibility of reports from high-stakes tests has made it clear that a school or district can no longer describe itself only in terms of teacher qualifications, professional development opportunities it provides, and new initiatives it promises. They must answer the question of whether those actions have made a positive difference for students. That is explored in the upcoming section, "Documenting Results" (page 42).

Before you can begin documenting impact on students, however, you need assurance that implementation is occurring consistently across the school. That assurance requires articulating the indicators of implementation in advance and planning how data will be gathered and reported. Evidence must also show that the time, energy, and money invested in the new strategies was worth it. In addition, the planning process must identify which assessments will document short-term and ongoing evidence of results for students.

The process of monitoring evidence of implementation consists simply of ensuring that, as the responsible adults in the school, we do what we say we will do. School improvement plans represent a set of commitments, and school leaders—teachers and administrators—need to make sure the planned actions happen. As Reeves (2006) points out, "The 'Foolproof Reading System' worked in some schools but did not in others. The 'Can't-Miss Math Program' succeeded one month and fell flat the next. The source of such inconsistencies is hardly a mystery, as the cause of success in improving student achievement is not the brand name of the product but the degree of implementation by the teacher" (p. 78).

The school improvement/leadership team must identify evidence that will demonstrate use of the schoolwide and classroom changes designated in the plan. Gathering this evidence should be an ongoing process to ensure the information is readily available—unlike the experiences of some schools that reach the end of a year or planning cycle and must frantically look backward, trying to retrieve and recapture documentation for reports and for next rounds of grant applications.

Ensuring implementation requires that the principal and staff:

- Identify indicators of implementation

- Participate in professional development needed for implementation

- Mutually agree on how data will be gathered to monitor implementation

- Review this data to identify internal expertise, respond to individual needs, and adjust timelines and professional development plans

What Data Are You Looking For?

This component of data use for ensuring implementation focuses on accountability for accomplishing the changes that staff have identified and affirmed.

A four-step process (Holcomb, 2012) helps ensure that expectations are clear to all and that evidence of implementation can be produced: (1) creating a shared understanding, (2) designing tools to document evidence of implementation, (3) designing the process by which that documentation can occur, and (4) generating reporting statements that summarize data and progress.

The first step defines what data you're looking for by making sure everyone has a shared image of what the innovation looks like in practice. Such "indicators of implementation" emerge as staff address the following questions:

1. What will implementation of this strategy *look* like?

    › What will teachers be doing?

    › How will that differ from what we do now?

    › What will we do more often, more consistently, and more rigorously?

    › What will teachers be doing less of or not doing? What are we leaving behind to make room for more powerful strategies?

> › What will students be doing that is different, more consistent, and more rigorous?

> › What artifacts will be observable in the school or classroom (materials, manipulatives, student work samples, and so on)?

2. What will implementation of the strategy *sound* like?

> › What terminology and phrases should all teachers be using?

> › Will the classroom be quiet or filled with productive noise?

> › What will students be talking about and saying?

Curriculum designers and program publishers often include criteria or checklists for implementation. Helpful items from these resources should be connected to the specific, authentic questions in the preceding list.

How Will You Find the Data?

The next two steps are designing the *tools* with which to document the evidence of implementation and the *process* by which that documentation can occur. Teacher involvement in this planning is essential to make a clear distinction between ensuring the success of the school improvement plan and the formal evaluation of individual teachers.

A typical method of gathering implementation data is the school and classroom walkthrough, in which administrators, teacher leaders, and colleagues make note of these specific chosen indicators (not a prepackaged, multipage plethora of items) and compile a count of the frequency of occurrence. However, Douglas Reeves (2006) suggests that "effective monitoring include not only frequency but also the specification of levels of implementation" (p. 78). He defines implementation as "the degree to which the specific elements of school improvement processes are implemented at the student and classroom levels" and describes effective implementation not only as present or absent but as "a continuous variable . . . [with] degrees of successful implementation that are subject to quantitative and narrative description" (p. 78). For complex changes, a continuum can be outlined by developing an Innovation Configuration Map (Holcomb, 2012).

The fourth step is generating drafts of *reporting statements* that will summarize the data and capture the progress being made. Looking ahead, the principal, the school improvement/leadership team, and data team should ask, "What does the school want to be able to report?" Reporting statements can be drafted with blanks left in them for data to be added later. For example, a statement like "Asking questions to check for understanding was observed in _____ percent of classroom drop-ins in September and rose to _____ percent in April," is much more accurate and useful than "All teachers were trained in questioning techniques." It also helps to identify the type of tools and processes that will be needed to provide the data.

Following are additional examples of statements that can capture evidence of implementation. The italicized words can be replaced to match the strategies of the actual school improvement plan.

- *All* staff members completed initial training in *cooperative learning strategies*.

- *Eighty-five percent* of classroom walkthroughs showed evidence of *planning tools used before writing*.

- *Every* grade level has *at least five unit plans with differentiation strategies* on file in the teacher resource center.

- *Parent attendance at conferences* increased from *45 percent* to *75 percent*.

- The percentage of teachers surveyed who *feel confident with hands-on math* increased from *58 percent* to *85 percent*.

How Will You Use the Data?

Just as overall data are analyzed to identify celebrations and concerns, the evidence of implementation is used for those same two purposes—to recognize not only evidence of implementation challenges but also evidence of implementation success. The principal must commend those who have been leading the way and those who have been the most successful with new practices or procedures so they know their efforts are recognized and they can maintain their motivation. These leaders can also become sources of internal expertise and support to their colleagues who may be struggling with the expectations. To address concerns, the principal may need to seek additional help from outside the school or identify individuals or grade-level teams with whom he or she can have personal conversations to better understand what is happening and what action is needed.

Documenting Results

The last of the six components of data use for school improvement involves planning how results for students will be documented. The desired impacts on students are not just academic. When priority areas and strategies include factors like staff relationships and student engagement, evidence from the affective domain is needed to demonstrate change. Some evidence shows up as the team checks the nonacademic student data (for example, attendance and behavior referrals) on an ongoing basis. Perceptual data from short questionnaires or focus groups may also be needed. Academic evidence requires review of the assessment framework of the district and school and may then entail selection or development of more or different assessments.

What Data Are You Looking For?

Evidence of teacher and school success with new instructional practices eventually appears in the large-scale assessments of student learning, but a whole year is a long time to wait and may not yield immediate validation. The anxiety of waiting for state results and the questions about whether those tests are fair, reasonable, valid, reliable, and so forth have created fertile ground for changing assessment practices and beliefs. Principals and teachers want to be able to predict how their students will do and to more accurately identify who needs help and on what specific concepts and skills. The work of Marzano (2010), Stiggins (2007), Stiggins, Arter, Chappuis, and Chappuis,

(2004), Reeves (2006, 2007), Guskey (2007), and others have encouraged the use of classroom data in real time.

Such evidence of impact on student learning requires the use of frequent academic data, which may not yet be available. Most of the data currently assembled and used by schools are *summative* data. As noted in chapter 1, high-performing schools and districts provide or develop *formative* assessments to balance large-scale, high-stakes tests. The *Learning from Leadership* study (Louis et al., 2010) further affirmed that high data-use schools use formative assessments of student progress at regular intervals throughout the year. This chapter describes an additional type of assessment— *benchmark* (or *interim*) *assessment*—with the focus on its relationship to documenting results of schoolwide efforts. Chapter 4 continues a more in-depth discussion of assessment frameworks in the context of teacher teams working together to plan instruction and to identify and support struggling students.

Documenting results of school improvement involves looking at data from all three types of assessment: (1) summative, (2) benchmark/interim, and (3) formative. At least one set of summative data come automatically from your state. You and your colleagues will be instrumental in working with your district to identify the full assessment framework that will yield more frequent, accessible evidence of student progress.

Summative data represent snapshots of a point in time of a student's learning. Examples include a test given at the end of a unit or course or a standardized test (for example, state assessment) given once a year. The purpose of these tests is typically to measure student learning in general rather than to provide immediate feedback to the specific student or teacher. A standardized test often provides only a score, percentile, or proficiency level as feedback to students. Teachers use the results of large-scale summative assessments to make changes for the next school year, but they rarely find them to be helpful with instructional planning for the next week.

Benchmark, or interim, assessments are given periodically to provide diagnostic information and/or to show progress over a portion of the school year. These may be commercial products like the Measures of Academic Progress (MAP) tests or Read 180 tests, which many schools give in the fall, winter, and spring. Benchmark assessments may also be developed locally, based on state standards and district curricula. Results are sometimes used as an indicator when quarterly progress reports are provided to students and parents.

Formative data from more frequent assessments have emerged in a virtual revolution to counter the misuses of large-scale, standardized tests. Fullan (2005) refers to assessment for learning as "one of the most high-yield strategies to come on the scene" and describes it as high yield "in the sense that it represents a powerful strategy for changing teaching and learning, and is learnable within reasonable time frames" (p. 54). He then summarizes the research of Black, Wiliam, and associates, which addresses four areas of classroom teaching and learning: (1) questioning, (2) feedback through grades, (3) peer- and self-assessment by students, and (4) the formative use of summative tests. Black himself states that the improvements documented for most participating teachers were of such significance that "if replicated across the whole school, they would raise the performance of a school at the twenty-fifth percentile of achievement nationally into the upper half" (as cited in Fullan, 2005, p. 54).

How Will You Find the Data?

The search for data to document results on nonacademic improvement goals (for example, discipline and climate) occurs at the building level. The indicators of implementation and the evidence mentioned in SMART goals provide clues about where to look for that information.

Identification of data to document results in student learning on a frequent basis requires a collaborative effort between the school (or all elementary schools in a large district) and the central office. The flow of data already available to schools may include systemwide benchmark or interim assessments such as the Measures of Academic Progress (MAP) tests. Districts may also expect schools to use certain curriculum-based assessments to track student progress. The principal plays a key role in bridging school initiatives with the district context. Where gaps exist and development of common formative assessments is needed, the principal also provides influence on the district to engage teachers from all schools in common grade-level work that strengthens the connections between professionals and provides vertical consistency for the instructional program.

How Will You Use the Data?

In the context of schoolwide improvement, evidence of student learning must be used to help staff maintain diligent implementation and to identify celebrations and concerns. In the case of a benchmark assessment of reading level, the school might report, "Our percentage of students reading at grade level went from 67 percent in the fall to 79 percent on the winter administration." Other statements of impact might include:

- The percentage of students proficient and above in _____ on the _____ improved from _____ percent to _____ percent.

- Our mean score on the _____ improved from the _____ percentile to the _____ percentile.

- The number of students completing _____ percent of their assignments on time improved from _____ to _____ .

- The average per-student gain from fall to spring was _____ points.

Intentional planning for schoolwide awareness and celebration of ongoing student progress was evident early in the year at Rockwood Elementary in Oklahoma City, Oklahoma. Even though it was only the third week of school, two bulletin boards were already prepared to serve as their data walls. One wall had been divided into sections with headings for each of the upcoming assessments: comprehensive benchmark 1 (district assessment), quarter benchmark 1 (district), quarter benchmark 2 (district), fifth-grade writing (state), and so on. Green, yellow, and red rows across the bulletin board were ready for data to be posted to note student levels of proficiency. The other bulletin board was labeled the DIBELS (Dynamic Indicators of Basic Early Literacy Skills) Data Wall;

each section was identified with a teacher's name and contained a strip of green, yellow, and red paper. Once DIBELS testing had occurred, students decorated stick figures to represent themselves and placed their stick figure on the green, yellow, or red strip to indicate their level. Even though figures did not display their names (for privacy and dignity), students recognized their own stick figure, knew their status, and worked to move their figure to a higher level on the next assessment.

Your Role as Principal

This chapter has described how data use can provide a critical support for school improvement efforts, but data-use initiatives must be accompanied by hard, focused work, because "the leap from data to action is not simple" (Knapp et al., 2006, p. 18). As school leader, perhaps the most difficult—and most necessary—part of your job is ensuring that this work happens. The reproducible chart on page 46, Components of Data Use, summarizes key questions and tasks related to each component of data use in schoolwide decision making.

Some of these processes can be handled completely at the building level. Others, such as selection or development of appropriate formative assessments, must be based on a thorough understanding of the district's assessment framework as well as on knowledge of the people and processes involved in advocating for the modifications and additions needed to support your school and students. As a result, you may find it helpful to make your journal notes for this chapter in two columns: "district" and "school."

The National Association of Elementary School Principals (NAESP, 2008) points out that "effective leaders are skilled at focusing on the most important data and bringing it to the forefront so it can be analyzed to inform changes that make sense for the school's staff and community" (p. 99). The most visible of these changes are those that affect the entire school and are captured in documents such as school improvement plans that are accessible to the public and may be evaluated by the state and district. It would be highly unusual to discover that your school is currently making complete use of all the aspects of data use described here. If you are, your goal should be submitting a journal article and a proposal to present at your national conference. If you are not, do not be discouraged or overwhelmed at this point.

Your reflections should include a complete list of all the things that need attention over time, so you have complete data from which to prioritize for your goal-setting in chapter 6. Remember that the good leader is not the one with a grandiose plan trying to do everything at once but the one who makes wises decisions about what provides the greatest leverage to accomplish what students need the school to do. Most importantly, schools—and especially you as the school's leader—must constantly look around and ask, "Can we demonstrate that what we are doing is having a positive impact on students?"

Components of Data Use

Assembling the Data	• What's available and in use? • What's available and not in use? • Of the data available but not in use, prioritize what to introduce in order to answer the questions under "Analyzing Current Status." • Employ the snowball approach to introducing other new data.
Analyzing Current Status	• Are we "walking the talk" of our mission—putting our goals into action? Look for data that would provide evidence of the key phrases. • Does the school have smoldering issues that need to be viewed more objectively? Look for evidence to confirm or contradict the prevailing positions. • Drill down for student learning data related to the most essential concepts and skills.
Assessing Current Efforts	• List all change initiatives under way in your school. • Which are working as intended? • Which seem to be stuck? Why might that be? • Identify existing efforts to stop, refine, sustain, or replace current efforts.
Determining Next Steps	• Set priorities based on a summary of the findings about current status. • Study underlying factors related to priorities. • Research effective practices that match the specific needs in your data. • List the initiatives being continued as well as new efforts to be initiated. • Test whether the combination of strategies will respond to the specific needs and engage all staff.
Ensuring Implementation	• Identify indicators of implementation. • Provide professional development needed for implementation. • Mutually agree on how data will be gathered to monitor implementation. • Use data to identify internal expertise, respond to individual needs, and adjust timeliness and professional development plans.
Documenting Results	• Articulate the intended effects of the strategies chosen. • What assessments will capture those effects? What assessments need to be added? • How will information about student progress be recorded and reported?

4

Data to Support Struggling Students

Chapter 3 described the principal's role in working with his or her school improvement/leadership team, data team, and entire staff to analyze data, evaluate current efforts, and determine next steps for school improvement. Those discussions inevitably surface concerns about students who are not on pace to master necessary skills and who struggle for a variety of reasons. It would be unusual to find a school improvement plan that did not include some wording like "develop a schoolwide support system for struggling learners" among its strategies. The principal's leadership responsibilities become even more focused on students and teachers in this chapter and the next. Here we discuss instructional leadership at the whole-school level, which includes coordinating the times and methods of support for struggling learners. Chapter 5 moves the focus to strengthening instruction at the individual classroom level.

Some sites use the term *professional learning communities* (PLCs; Hord, 2003; Hord & Sommers, 2008) or the trademarked phrase "Professional Learning Communities at Work" (DuFour et al., 2010) to describe a structure and process by which teachers work together to explore what they want students to know and be able to do, how they will assess those outcomes, and what they will do to support students who have not mastered the content after initial instruction. The reality is that supporting struggling students begins at the individual classroom level, but individual teachers cannot cope with this demand in isolation. Without collaboration and support from colleagues, the teachers of struggling students may wind up as struggling teachers. Many schools, districts, and states use the specific term *response to intervention* (RTI) to describe their support system for struggling students, and this chapter includes a section explaining this approach.

Teacher Collaboration

Chapter 1 highlighted the important need for opportunities for teacher collaboration in creating a data-friendly school culture. Real-life examples of ways in which elementary teachers have joined up to plan instruction and support for students include:

- Grade-level teams

- Co-teaching combinations of general education and special education teachers

- All teachers of a grade level and the teachers who support them (for example, staff members who work with special education students, English learners [ELs], and gifted students)

- Grade-level teachers and media specialists

- Grade-level team leaders, reading and math coaches, paraprofessionals, and parents

- Cross-district teams of like content, linked by videoconferencing (for example, in small rural districts)

- Enrichment teams of classroom teachers joined by extended learning specialists, technology integration specialists, and library media specialists

True collaboration, however, is more than a structure. Hargreaves (2009) describes how such combinations of teachers

> have sharpened collaborative cultures by adding a clear school focus and providing performance data to guide teachers' joint reflections, discussions, and decisions, and to connect them to student achievement. . . . They are living communities and lively cultures dedicated to improving the life and learning of students and adults where data inform but do not drive judgments about practice. . . . And members of the community care not just about the outcomes of their short-term teams, but about each other as people because they are in a long-term relationship. (p. 31)

Sound working relationships develop the kind of trust necessary to remain open about both the learning struggles of the students and the teaching struggles of the professionals. One way to build trust among teachers is by helping them work together on authentic tasks, such as the one described by Reeves (2004) in the next section. By focusing on the most essential concepts and skills, teachers begin to answer the question of what data they are looking for.

What Data Are You Looking For?

As mentioned in chapter 3, summative data can alert the school to general needs that must be addressed on a schoolwide basis, but more specific data are needed to plan instruction and support struggling students. This entails use of a daily flow of information that is skill-specific and student-specific.

Skill-Specific Data

If teachers are going to support struggling students with an eye toward closing achievement gaps, they cannot employ packaged programs or place students in ability groups that will make them re-cover all aspects of a grade or unit. With limited available contact time, students must receive help that is strategically targeted to missing skills. This kind of specific data cannot be tracked on each and every aspect of learning encompassed in voluminous state standards. Some prioritizing must occur through the use of the MECS and assessment frameworks.

Most Essential Concepts and Skills

Douglas Reeves (2004) describes a collaborative process by which some concepts and skills rise to the level of what he calls "power standards." He advises schools to:

- **Have faculty agree on the "twelve most important standards for each subject, each grade."** The way to accelerate this is to have teachers answer the question, What knowledge and skills do students need to acquire in the next lower grade in order to come into your class with confidence and success next year? Fifth-grade teachers, for example, may have difficulty narrowing the focus for their own grade-level curriculum, but they have little trouble in narrowing the focus of prerequisites for students coming from fourth grade into their classrooms.

- **Have faculty teams design very short assessments that address these brief sets of power standards over the course of a year.** "Very short" means about fifteen items: twelve multiple choice and three extended response. This should take no more than twenty minutes of classroom time each month, and the grading can be immediate.

- **Provide some time in faculty meetings or already scheduled group time to quickly grade the three extended-response items.** Ensure that the credit given is consistent; that is, faculty members can look at an anonymous piece of student work and agree on whether it is proficient and what credit it should receive.

- **Provide time in faculty meetings after each assessment has been graded to get very clear answers to this question.** Based on the results we have just observed, how will the next few weeks be different in schedule, curriculum, and teaching strategies?

When central office staff help coordinate this type of process by grade-level teachers from across the district, vertical and horizontal articulation is achieved. Every district should also have an assessment framework grounded in a set of most essential skills and concepts.

Assessment Frameworks

Even before No Child Left Behind changed from testing one elementary grade to testing yearly in grades 3–8, state standards were usually backward mapped to describe more specific grade-level expectations. In many places, these are still too numerous and cumbersome to be used for determining which assessments will provide skill-specific data at the student level.

The principal is a critical link between school and district, and his or her knowledge of the assessments already in place is a prerequisite to knowing where gaps exist that need to be filled. The reproducible Assessment Framework Template on page 66 can be used to summarize the summative, benchmark (interim), and formative assessment practices currently in place for any one content area.

For example, a principal might begin with three such assessment worksheets—one for reading, one for math, and one for writing. From his or her unique position, the principal consults with district personnel and with grade-level teams at the site to chart the types of assessments that all teachers are expected to use and that various teachers have developed in groups or individually.

Classroom-level assessment practices should not be regarded as synonymous with *tests*. Real-time information on how students are succeeding includes observing what they are doing, listening to their questions, polling them for their own description of how well they understand, and so on. *Testing* happens at specific times, and it is true that it can take too much time. *Assessment* is a constant, ongoing part of the interaction between teacher and student and should not be measured as a separate act. While a distinction may exist between teaching and *testing*, the relationship between teaching and *assessing* should be seamless.

In response to the concern that addition of formative assessments will cause over-testing, Reeves (2006) counters:

> Schools are, indeed, over-tested if we define tests as summative, evaluative, provided at the end of the year, and accompanied by feedback that is woefully late and inherently useless. But schools are under-*assessed*. Assessments in contrast to tests, are formative, provided during the year, designed to improve teaching and learning, and accompanied by immediate feedback. (p. 86, italics added)

Reeves describes the Broad Prize–winning district of Norfolk, Virginia, which assesses at least quarterly and often every other week. Feedback in this district is "typically provided the day after the assessment, sometimes the same day . . . [and] results include not only the scores for each student but a detailed item and cluster analysis, used for planning instruction the following week" (p. 86).

Formative assessments need to be carefully planned to address two goals. The first goal is to accurately assess student learning and to provide direction for instruction. A variety of traditional methods can be used, ranging from multiple-choice tests, written assignments, and projects to nontraditional methods such as games and panel discussions. The traditional methods provide individual feedback and scores, while the nontraditional methods provide immediate feedback but not individual scores. Another method to provide additional information on individual and class progress is for the students to maintain journals that teachers periodically review. Other examples of formative assessments include practice tests and essays. Even a pop quiz, given a few days prior to the unit test, can serve as a formative assessment. Additional strategies for formative assessment include peer grading and self-reflection.

Literacy Assessment in the Early Grades

One of the unique challenges at the elementary level is the lack of schoolwide assessment data from grades K–2. This is not to say that even more students should participate in high-stakes, large-scale tests. It *is* to say that schools and districts need to determine how they will diagnose needs and monitor progress in these critical early years. The nature of the skills and the developmental stages of young children both suggest that performance assessment, observation, and anecdotal evidence are appropriate and necessary. However, those same factors can contribute to lack of consistency as individual teachers make idiosyncratic decisions about how to determine profi-ciency. Teachers must work together using common criteria, and the district must help shape their work. The district must also ensure that foundational skills in primary grades are appropriately assessed and that data are purposefully collected and aggregated to begin the flow of information about student progress through the elementary years.

For example, a commercial reading test that provides information about a student's reading level but no other diagnostic information may tell teachers what they already know: the child is way below grade level. Teachers need information about the specific skills that must be strengthened to accelerate the individual student's reading ability.

Two common approaches to reading assessment that yield helpful information are the DIBELS tests and running records with miscue analysis. This book does not endorse any commercial prod-uct but uses these two only as examples of the kinds of assessment decisions that need to be made in conjunction with the district.

Many struggling schools who received Reading First funding (when it was still available) used DIBELS tests to meet grant requirements, but they often abandoned the assessment when the funding expired. Even when the tests were given, the thoroughness with which they were used to plan instruction varied widely. These assessments are individualized and standardized measures of early literacy development. Teachers use the short, one-minute fluency measures of DIBELS to monitor the development of their students' early reading skills. DIBELS measures also assess a reader's knowledge of initial sounds, letter naming, phoneme segmentation, nonsense words, oral reading, retelling, and word use. Teachers can use the results of the assessment to measure indi-vidual student progress and to determine how an individual student compares with peers.

However, researchers Schilling, Carlisle, Scott, and Zeng (2007) caution that DIBELS should be used in conjunction with other assessments because DIBELS may understate problems some chil-dren are having with comprehension. In one New Mexico district, teachers of the early grades use this comprehensive approach: DIBELS testing three times a year is supplemented with frequent one-minute assessments to monitor progress. Teachers use the data to adjust instruction for their students. In addition, grade-level teams meet at least monthly to discuss data from these assess-ments (Olson, 2007). A new version of the assessment, DIBELS Next, now includes a comprehension measure as well. It is a *cloze assessment* in which the students read a passage and choose new words to replace words that have been omitted. Although somewhat simplistic, it does provide insight into student knowledge of which substitute word makes the most sense in the context of the passage.

For inexperienced readers who do not yet read and write conventionally, *process-oriented assess-ments* include observations of what they do as they attempt to read and write. During reading, teachers may note how the child is holding a book, "reading" the illustrations, or noticing print. During writing, teachers may observe the interactions that occur as children write with others and may ask children about the meaning of their work.

For students who have made the transition into reading, running records with miscue analy-sis can be essential to understanding their reading process. *Running records* are diagnostic notes the teacher makes as a child reads aloud a passage from a text. Using a series of checkmarks for words read correctly and notations for words incorrectly omitted, inserted, or misread, the running record provides a wealth of information to the teacher about the student as a reader. Running records help teachers note a child's reading fluency—phrasing, smoothness, and pace when reading a text. The observation also provides the teacher with information about the child's reading habits and comfort level with the text. After collecting a running record of the students' reading process, teachers can analyze the errors the reader made. This process, called *miscue analysis*, helps teachers understand the ways in which their students read texts. Throughout the school year, multiple running records with miscue analysis provide a clear picture of what children do as they are engaged in reading.

Informal reading inventories (IRIs) are informal assessments teachers administer to understand student progress in reading and writing. They are often administrated three times during an academic school year—at the beginning of the school year to obtain baseline data, during the middle of the year to chart progress, and at the end of the year to note literacy growth. During these assessments, students read passages orally and silently and answer comprehension questions about the passage. When students read orally, the teacher takes running records and notes the readers' fluency. The teacher then evaluates the student as a reader in order to match the student with texts that he or she can read independently or with instructional assistance.

Such techniques provide teachers with immediate feedback that can be used to improve and adjust the instructional methods they use with individual children and to determine how they form small groups for skill instruction.

Assessment in Mathematics

The focus of research on early literacy was supported by many national projects, among which Reading First grants were a significant influence. As a result, more emphasis was placed on selection of "approved" reading assessments. Mathematics, however, has come to the fore at the elementary level in more recent iterations of No Child Left Behind. Most of the assessments used for skill-specific information come from curriculum-based assessments and reflect some local philosophy about mathematics. For example, if the adopted math program is a traditional, computation-oriented program, assessments reflect that focus. If the math program is more hands-on and aimed toward concept attainment, more authentic assessments and observational tools may be provided. School staff members must be involved in district committees that align the MECS with curriculum materials and assessments in order to ensure that data about both computational skills and conceptual understanding are or will be available and parallel the ways in which students are assessed by the state.

Student-Specific Data

Aligning assessments with the most essential concepts and skills and providing a balance of summative, benchmark, and formative data ensure an assessment framework capable of providing skill-specific information. Classroom teachers further need to know whether all children in the class are progressing toward those key objectives or whether some children need instruction in specific areas and what those areas are. According to the Connecticut State Department of Education (2000),

> Assessment can assist the teacher in planning flexible groups and in determining which children need more instruction—or, conversely, a greater level of challenge—in a particular competency or set of competencies. Because individual children will acquire various competencies at different rates, ongoing assessment is necessary for re-evaluating children's needs and reconstituting flexible groups on a regular basis. (p. 59)

Unfortunately, it may not be easy for teachers to find ongoing data to evaluate children's needs and form flexible groups. As the next section indicates, new forms of assessment and new ways of recording student learning may be necessary.

How Will You Find the Data?

In order to support struggling students, groups of teachers need to know more than how many students are not meeting proficiency levels and which skills represent the lowest performance on a standardized test. Teachers need to know, student by student, which skills represent gaps in their development. Teachers typically do not have this kind of information, which is why new forms of assessment and new forms of teacher record keeping may be needed.

New Forms of Assessment

No single assessment tool can provide a complete picture of a child's progress or achievement. Additionally, no single test can meet the needs of all groups who require information about school and student performance. Multiple forms of assessment, many of which can occur as part of instructional situations, help illuminate patterns of a child's learning behavior. These assessments include informal assessments, formal assessments, and authentic assessments. When combined as a comprehensive snapshot of a student's literacy growth, these multiple assessments provide valuable information for teachers as they work to meet the learning needs of individual students.

According to Marshall (2006a), such assessments yield the following benefits and uses:

- Give teachers timely insights on the kinds of minute-by-minute classroom adjustments that might immediately resolve student misconceptions and misunderstandings and prevent them from continuing week after week

- Give teachers periodic feedback on whether their students are actually learning what's being taught—specifically what's working and what isn't working in the way they are orchestrating learning experiences

- Give teachers feedback on ways to improve their unit and lesson planning for better student understanding and retention

- Provide fine-grained data for teacher teams to analyze student learning results and to plan improvements

- Identify students who need follow-up and the areas in which they need extra help, including skills and concepts that need to be retaught to the whole class, to small groups, or to individual students

New Forms of Teacher Record Keeping

Authentic and collaborative use of formative assessment inevitably leads to discussion of the question, What should we be keeping track of? Many other authors—Marzano, Reeves, Stiggins, Guskey, O'Connor, and more—have explored the issues of grading and reporting in greater depth than this book allows. Traditional practice has been to record numbers of points for various activities and assignments and average them together into a letter grade. This naturally results in students focusing on how to get more points or how to raise their grade. At the same time, teachers wonder why students aren't intrinsically motivated to learn for learning's sake.

Teachers who examine student work together and use formative assessments ask different questions and keep track of student progress in different ways. They have collaborative discussions about specific students and specific skills. Before determining that a student is not successful, they ask, "What other data do we have for this student related to these same skills?" Before averaging the student's worst and best performances to assign a mean grade, they ask, "What is our most recent evidence of his or her level of proficiency?"

Keeping in mind the very real constraints of time—especially teacher time—is obviously important. Thus while some approaches to data collection and analysis may, by their nature, require fairly intensive investments of time, other approaches can be easy to implement while providing helpful data. Depka (2006) suggests that teachers use color-coding when recording low scores in a grade book. The use of the different color "creates a visual of those in need of occasional support and identifies students who are experiencing repeated difficulties" (p. 69). This visual can be helpful to the teacher when planning instruction and can also provide data for teacher-principal meetings on student progress or for a discussion among teachers working to identify additional strategies to use with students having difficulty.

Figure 4.1 provides a glimpse of a more comprehensive approach that the teacher can keep as a page for each student in the teacher's computer or three-ring binder. The items on the left represent the MECS for sixth-grade math. This short list of the most essential benchmarks has been broken down so students and teachers know exactly what to work on. For example, the originally stated benchmark indicated that the student will be able to add, subtract, multiply, and divide using decimals. In figure 4.1, the four operations have been separated into separate rows to better target the student's zone of proximal development.

The circle with four quadrants in the first column represents four proficiency levels, which may be aligned with the state's proficiency levels or with any four-point scale or rubric. The column heading "Most Recent Evidence" indicates that this simple graphic will not be an average. It will show the student's *current* status as the quadrants are shaded, based on formative assessments, actual student work, or observation during class. In the example given in figure 4.1, it is early in the year, and the first assessment was a quiz given on September 15. The student reached proficiency

Sixth-Grade Math

Name of Student _____

Benchmarks	Most Recent Evidence	Evidence of Progress							
Add decimals	(circle: 4 1 / 3 2 — 3 and 2 shaded)	9/15 Quiz 3							
Subtract decimals	(circle: 4 1 / 3 2 — 2 shaded)	9/15 Quiz 2							
Multiply decimals	(circle: 4 1 / 3 2)								
Divide decimals	(circle: 4 1 / 3 2)								
Add fractions with like denominators	(circle: 4 1 / 3 2)								
Add fractions with unlike denominators	(circle: 4 1 / 3 2)								
Add mixed numbers, like denominators	(circle: 4 1 / 3 2)								

Figure 4.1 Individual academic progress chart.

on adding decimals but missed some of the items related to subtracting decimals. Entries in the remaining columns will show progress toward mastery from various sources as the teacher formally and informally assesses the respective skill.

In many settings, teachers begin by working with grade-level colleagues at the site level to create their own spreadsheets, similar to figure 4.1. These discussions provide valuable information and support for instructional planning and motivating students. Unfortunately, if the district still requires a traditional report card, even the teacher leaders who most value and advocate for standards-based record keeping say that it is time-consuming because they have to keep "two sets of books" or records in order to enter the data the district requires and have the information they want for authentic use. Because grading and reporting policies are determined at the district level, this raises another area for the principal's role in bringing his or her school's influence to bear on district policy and practice.

How Will You Use the Data?

When teachers have skill-specific and student-specific information, they can keep track of precisely who knows (and doesn't know) which of the most essential concepts and skills. They can use these data in three very powerful ways:

1. To engage students in their own learning

2. To plan and differentiate classroom instruction

3. To work with colleagues to provide systems of support beyond their individual classroom walls

Using Data to Engage Students

A powerful benefit of formative assessments is that they can be used to provide meaningful feedback to students. One approach is to discuss the items on a test. This discussion goes beyond simply giving the correct answer to explaining why the answer is correct and why other responses are incorrect. Students should be involved in the discussion to encourage them to reflect on the information.

A second way to utilize formative data and to support learners is through peer tutoring. Students in the class pair up and then grade their work together and discuss the correct answers and any errors that occurred, explaining the correct answers. A third approach is for students to grade their own work and then write explanations for the correct and incorrect responses. Gregory and Kuzmich (2004) suggest teachers encourage students to self-assess their work using teacher-provided rubrics—and then use the data they collect to decide how to improve their current product or what to do differently on their next attempt.

In his work on classroom assessment, Rick Stiggins (2007) describes the importance of "a series of interlaced experiences that enhance the learning process by keeping students confident and focused on their progress, even in the face of occasional setbacks" (p. 23). He describes characteristics of the process in which teachers enhance, rather than merely monitor, their students' learning. First, teachers share achievement targets with the students, providing the benchmarks in student-friendly language and showing them examples of high-quality work. Second, they engage students in frequent self-assessments that provide descriptive feedback related to specific skills and in small amounts they can digest. Third, they help students use this feedback to chart their progress and set goals. Stiggins notes that "the students' role is to understand what success looks like, to use feedback from each assessment to discover where they are ... and to determine how to do better next time" (p. 23).

Michael Fullan (2009) also takes a broad view of students as self-assessors. Describing student roles in the context of a large-scale literacy initiative in Ontario, he includes:

- Knowing and understanding what they are expected to learn

- Identifying their own strengths, needs, and interests

- Reflecting on their progress and setting goals

- Taking steps to improve their literacy learning

- Writing nonfiction with ease and coherence

- Advocating for themselves

Citing their ability to now write nonfiction with ease and coherence, Fullan emphasizes that he is not talking about just passing a test. The students have accomplished a skill that they can transfer, one that will enable them to be more successful in every content area. As they advocate for themselves, they can describe what they need to learn and provide input on how they demonstrate their acquired knowledge and skill. For example, teachers may provide students with green and red cards that represent whether they understand the discussion points or whether they have the correct answer for a problem (green) or don't (red). "Raising the red flag" can become a comfortable way for students to state their need for further explanation. "Exit cards" given to the teacher at the end of a class period can be used to identify a key question or point that was missed or to simply record a numerical code, such as 4 = got it, great; 3 = doing OK; 2 = got parts of it and I'll try; or 1 = really need help before I can go any further. These examples give students opportunities to communicate how well they are learning during and after the introduction of new content.

Using Data to Plan and Differentiate Classroom Instruction

At its heart, assessment is a continuing process in which both teachers and students use information to guide the next steps in learning. For the student, assessment provides feedback on understanding. Results of a test or comments on a written assignment help him or her answer questions such as, Am I getting it? and How am I doing? Assessments can help teachers answer related questions, such as, Which students are learning? Similarly, an analysis of the results can help a teacher pinpoint specific difficulties or misconceptions to further explain or correct. Teachers can also use assessments for diagnostic purposes. When applied to the class, the data can answer such questions as, Is the class ready for a new unit? Reviewing assessment information for an individual student helps teachers decide who needs additional help—and what type of help—as well as who can move on.

The characteristics that describe effective use of data to guide instruction in the classroom include:

- Assessment is embedded and ongoing and provides prompt, user-friendly feedback so adjustments can be made as needed, rather than just reported at the end of each learning-improvement cycle.

- Day-to-day classroom assessments emphasize formative assessments—information that provides early indication of whether learning is taking place—to minimize problems that might arise if learning barriers are not promptly identified and addressed.

- Day-to-day classroom assessments include qualitative data such as information from classroom observation as well as quantitative measures.

- Students are told the purpose of an assessment and how this information will be used.

Gregory and Kuzmich (2004) use the term "diagnostic teaching" and emphasize that "true diagnostic thinking requires teachers to reflect consciously on student learning and then connect their conclusions to the most effective next steps" (p. 52). Teachers using this diagnosis as a tool to improve their teaching collect data that allow them to answer these questions:

- What do I know about my students now?
- What is the nature and content of the final assessment for this unit or period of time?
- What don't I know about the content knowledge, the critical thinking, and the process or skill demonstration of my students? (p. 56)

One elementary school used a graphic display of data to keep the focus on children's progress. Hundreds of color-coded cards grouped by grade level lined the "assessment wall" in the office. Each card represented a student (names on the back for privacy purposes) and recorded his or her progress through the formative assessments that were given. Teachers met twice a month to review status and progress. They grouped and regrouped pupils according to the progress they were making, identified pupils below grade level, and most important, exchanged intervention strategies to help those who were struggling.

Using Data to Provide Schoolwide Systems of Support

With data available on specific skills for each student, teachers can adjust lesson plans—sometimes with little tweaks, sometimes with major shifts—to improve instruction for an entire class or for one child. Some of these changes may happen in the classroom. At other times, a student may need additional supports outside the scope of his or her regular classroom. This increased support is now frequently referred to as *response to intervention*.

Response to Intervention

Federal mandates since 2000 stimulated progress in the use of disaggregated data as a check for equity of access and achievement, especially related to race and poverty. During this same time-frame, the Individuals with Disabilities Education Improvement Act (IDEIA) of 2004 increased requirements for general education to support students with exceptional challenges. Response to intervention was created as "an organizational framework for instructional and curricular decisions and practices based upon students' responses . . . to integrate assessment and intervention within a multi-level prevention system to maximize student achievement and reduce behavior problems" (DuFour et al., 2010, p. 19).

Response to intervention is defined by Hall (2008) as "a dynamic problem-solving process in which data are integral in making decisions about what skills struggling readers lack, and whether instruction provided has been effective" (p. 17).

Purpose of RTI

Viewed from the perspective of broad goals, response to intervention is intended to ensure that low-performing students receive support in a timely manner. Procedures embedded in RTI include the following:

> Begin by ensuring that the general education classroom is providing effective instruction and assessment for all students. RtI then offers a way to bridge gaps between general and special education services by providing scientifically based interventions quickly and efficiently for all students who need support, before going through a lengthy process to determine eligibility for special education. (Brown-Chidsey, 2007)

While the initial emphasis of RTI is on successfully addressing the instructional needs of as many students as possible in the regular classroom—and without going through the process of establishing eligibility for special education before students can receive more intensive instruction—some students will need special education services. RTI "can provide schools with much-needed help to better distinguish between the truly disabled and those who might seem to need special education, but who really don't" (Fuchs as cited in Walser, 2007).

Levels in RTI

Response to intervention models are often illustrated with a triangle or pyramid that refers to *levels* or *tiers*. The first tier includes modifications teachers make in the regular classroom as they observe students, assist them, and differentiate instruction. A second tier includes additional time and support, such as small-group tutoring, for students who have not "responded" to classroom instruction by achieving proficiency. The third tier is reserved for students who still do not "respond" and need more intense intervention, such as formal evaluation, diagnosis, and preparation of an individualized education plan.

In Brown-Chidsey's description (2007), Tier 1 includes universal instruction and assessment of all students—in other words, the general education curriculum. Schools need to ensure that instruction and assessment are research-based and effective in helping students gain academic proficiency.

Success at Tier 1 is defined as the student demonstrating the levels of knowledge and skill expected for his or her age and grade.

Tier 1 is also referred to as *primary prevention* because it includes services that are in place for all students to support positive academic, behavioral, and mental health outcomes. Tier 1 in RTI involves a high-quality school and classroom environment, scientifically sound core curriculum and instruction, and intentional instructional practices. In Tier 1, school personnel must objectively and systematically evaluate whether their core curriculum materials are of sufficient quality and are backed by research. School staff must also evaluate teachers' instructional methods to make sure their teaching techniques adhere to sound instructional practice and are delivered as intended by the curriculum or intervention program.

To verify whether students are making adequate progress toward basic academic goals, it is imperative to gather data on the entire student population. In Tier 1, schoolwide assessments are conducted to gauge students' performance in the core academic areas (for example, reading and mathematics). All students are typically assessed three times per year (typically, fall, winter, and spring) beginning in kindergarten. The purpose of conducting schoolwide assessments is to gather critical data about all students and to identify individuals and groups who are not making satisfactory progress and are at risk for academic or behavioral problems. Students who are not mastering basic academic skills may require additional or different forms of instruction. Systematic reviews of assessment data are often carried out by collaborative instructional support teams, which usually consist of a multidisciplinary team of school personnel, such as general and special education teachers, principal, school counselor, school psychologist, and other related services personnel. Everything in chapters 3 and 4 pertaining to the use of formative assessment, diagnostic teaching, and flexible grouping supports Tier 1 general education instruction and differentiation.

According to Brown-Chidsey (2007), Tier 2 includes selected instructional activities and assessments for students who have not achieved the expected level while participating in Tier 1. An example of Tier 2 intervention is providing thirty minutes a day of additional reading or math instruction to first-grade students who have not met grade-level benchmarks. Teachers monitor students receiving Tier 2 support weekly to assess whether their skills are improving. If their assessment data indicate progress, the students gradually receive less support until they are able to succeed within the general education (Tier 1) program. If they do not make progress after a specified period of Tier 2 instruction, the school either adjusts the student's Tier 2 instruction or refers her or him for more intense attention.

Tier 2 is also described as *secondary prevention* because it includes targeted academic and behavioral services for students who are considered at risk and for whom the universal instruction has not been sufficient. These students are flagged as being at risk through the assessment process. Services at Tier 2 are more intense and focused on the specific needs of a student or group of students. Examples of services at this second tier might include small-group instruction for either academic or behavioral needs, additional support, and involvement in remediation programs such as Title I. Students receive Tier 2 intervention in addition to the core curriculum.

Tier 2 not only involves the implementation of more targeted, systematic interventions, it also involves more frequent monitoring of student progress (often weekly) than at Tier 1 to determine student responsiveness to the interventions provided. Typically, those students who respond well to Tier 2 interventions and whose data demonstrate they are progressing at an acceptable rate return to the general education curriculum or to Tier 1, the intervention offered to all students.

Only at Tier 3 does the school take steps to determine whether a student has a disability that requires special education. At this stage, the school conducts a comprehensive evaluation of the student's skills, including the data obtained in Tiers 1 and 2, to determine why a student's performance significantly differs from that of other students of his or her age and grade and to decide what additional instructional supports the student needs (Brown-Chidsey, 2007).

The intervention-assessment sequence in Tier 3 is markedly more intensive and individualized, and teachers monitor progress even more frequently than in Tier 2. Current best practice in the field suggests that students who do not make adequate progress at Tiers 2 and 3 be further evaluated to rule out conditions such as intellectual disability or emotional disturbance. Persistent failure to make academic gains at Tiers 2 and 3 may substantiate the presence of a learning disability.

The National Center for Learning Disabilities (n.d.) advises educators to think of RTI as a series of steps. The first step is instruction in the general classroom. Screening tests given in the classroom reveal students at risk for reading and other learning difficulties. For example, testing may show that a student who has difficulty reading needs additional instruction in phonics. In the second step, the classroom teacher might handle the instruction. In other cases, someone who has expertise in reading and phonics might instruct the student and other students who have the same difficulty. Students who fail to respond to this instruction may then be considered for more specialized instruction in step three, where instruction may occur with greater frequency or duration. If the achievement difficulties persist, a team of educators from different fields (for example, reading or counseling) may complete a comprehensive evaluation to determine eligibility for special education and related services.

Concerns

Few would quarrel with a sequence of support for struggling students, but some unintended negative consequences have been observed in the implementation of RTI and need to be avoided. One concern is that *students* rather than *services* are being labeled, when the focus should be on a specific skill, not generalized to the student as a whole person. For example, the following conversation took place about a student who was introduced as a "heavy-duty Tier 2 child":

> "We have a great intervention plan in place for Raquelle. She'll go to class for the first twenty minutes and then to the math intervention group for thirty minutes. She'll be back in time for the whole-group reading, but then when they split up for groups, she can head to the computer lab for the online math program. During lunch, she can do her basic facts packet while the volunteer is watching the library, and in the afternoon she'll have the regular math period with her class."

> I had to ask some questions about Raquelle. "Is she on grade level in reading?"

"Well, no, but we made AYP in reading and we really have to get to AYP in math this year."

"What is Raquelle's favorite subject?"

"Hmm . . . she loves PE. But there are just some sacrifices she'll have to make so she can get proficient in math."

"How does Raquelle learn best?"

"I'd say she's a pretty social kid. Before school starts in the morning, she usually has a little group around her and she's always getting them organized for this, that, or the other."

What a great plan for Raquelle. She gets to miss her favorite subject, work on the computer and with a learning packet by herself when she's a social kid, have the whole-group instruction but not the small-group help in reading, and devote 2 1/2 hours of her school day to mathematics. Her teachers want to do right by her. Their grant doesn't provide a late bus, so her options are limited to the school day. But I can almost see the sparkle begin to dim in Raquelle's brown eyes.

Another concern is that the use of data to plan support for struggling students can unintentionally be misused. One error of commission is to characterize all members of a "special population" as the same, such as assuming that because AYP was not reached for African American students, a program should be designed specifically for black males, and all black males are then regarded as poor readers. An error of omission is to disregard the full range of school activities (such as extracurricular and social-based activities) that keep students engaged and motivated for the long haul, focusing only on the short-term need to increase test scores.

A third caution relates to the perception that RTI is just a more difficult process with barriers that hold students out of identification for special education services.

Still, schools have used key features of RTI for more than two decades. Educators may recognize the similarity between components of RTI and previous terminology such as pre-referral intervention model, mainstream assistance team model, school-based consultation team model, and problem-solving model (Horowitz, 2005). However, RTI is actually "a more comprehensive framework for providing instruction, related interventions, and targeted special education for students at risk. . . . RTI is a schoolwide process for bringing stronger alignment to the instruction and assessment practices of a school and is generally more proactive and comprehensive than the more reactive and individualized functions of pre-referral and child study teams" (Mellard & Johnson, 2008, p. 139).

Though the new IDEIA regulations fall short of mandating RTI as a method for identifying children with learning disabilities, they say that states "cannot require" the use of IQ tests to diagnose learning disabilities, and they permit states to use "alternate methods" such as RTI to identify learning disabilities. To support early intervention, the regulations allow up to 15 percent of federal special education funds to be used for this purpose in general education classrooms (Walser, 2007). In addition, IDEIA now states that data from progress monitoring can also be used as an alternative to the "discrepancy model" to determine whether a student is eligible for special education services. As Brown-Chidsey (2007) specified:

Schools are allowed to use evidence of a student's failure to respond to instructional interventions as part of the data documenting the presence of a specific learning disability.

While RTI has been given special status by IDEIA, "RtI is not a special education process but a general education initiative that fits within school improvement efforts" (Canter, Klotz, & Cowan, 2008, p. 12). Therefore, school efforts to implement the process require close collaboration among general and special education teachers.

Progress Monitoring

Progress monitoring is the set of assessment procedures for determining how much students are benefiting from classroom instruction. A fundamental assumption of education is that students will benefit from high-quality instruction and will learn and achieve the skills and content taught in the classroom. For students who are not responsive to classroom instruction, alternative interventions can be provided and the students' response to that instruction can be monitored.

Progress monitoring affords a valid and efficient tool for gauging the effectiveness of instruction, determining whether instructional modifications are necessary, and providing important information for eventual classification and placement decisions (Johnson, Mellard, Fuchs, & McKnight, 2006).

Johnson et al. (2006) categorize the assessment procedures of RTI into three broad groups: (1) schoolwide screening, (2) progress-monitoring procedures, and (3) diagnostic tests. Table 4.1 highlights distinguishing features of the three approaches and their alignment with the tiers of intervention.

Table 4.1: Purposes of Three Types of Assessment in RTI Models

	Screening	**Progress Monitoring**	**Diagnostic Tests**
Population	Schoolwide	Class/small group/student	Individual student
Uses	Broad index	Specific academic skill or behavioral target	Specific academic domains of knowledge, skills, or abilities
Frequency	Yearly/3X/monthly	≤3 weeks/weekly/daily	Yearly
Purpose	Identify students who are at risk	Regroup students	Identify specific student deficits
Focus	School focus	Student/class focus	Student focus
Instruction	Class/school instruction and curriculum decisions	Within intervention/ (curriculum/instructional)	Selecting curriculum and instructional methods
Implications	As first step for intervention planning	Continue to revise placement	Planning or specifying intervention

Source: Johnson, Mellard, Fuchs, & McKnight, 2006.

In summary, the purposes and criteria for effective use of progress monitoring to document results on student learning include the following:

- Assess the specific skills embodied in state and local academic standards

- Assess marker variables that have been demonstrated to lead to the ultimate instructional target

- Be sensitive to small increments of growth over time

- Be administered efficiently over short periods

- Be administered repeatedly (using multiple forms)

- Result in data that can be summarized in teacher-friendly data displays

- Be comparable across students

- Be applicable for monitoring an individual student's progress over time

- Be relevant to development of instructional strategies and use of appropriate curriculum that addresses the area of need. (Texas Reading First, 2007, p. 4)

Clearly, implementation of formative assessments such as those described in chapter 3 will also provide the needed data for progress monitoring in your response to intervention model—or in any other model of a schoolwide system of support for struggling learners.

Your Role as Principal

Your leadership in using data to support struggling students is both direct at the school level and indirect through your interactions with the district. In order to have skill-specific and student-specific data on a timely basis, the school and district must have identified the MECS for each grade level and developed an assessment framework that includes both summative and formative assessments. Make copies of the template on page 66 and fill in those charts for reading, math, and any other skill area of concern. Then consider the balance of large-scale and real-time assessments available for your school's use and make notes about gaps. Pay particular attention to the non-state-tested grades K–2 as well as to the common assessment expectations and practices that are in place. Note where gaps or ambiguities exist, and make them part of your discussions with the instructional departments at the district level. Support efforts to identify approaches to assessment that will yield useful data while keeping teacher time for administering, recording, and analyzing assessments to a minimum. (For example, some schools use hand-held electronic devices to record results from DIBELS assessment. The data are then transferred to a computer, with the analysis available on a web-based system.) Advocate for involvement of your teacher leaders on district projects and committees.

Consistent administration of formative assessments and use of the results to diagnose and support struggling students depend on your leadership at the building level. Conveying those expectations and scheduling time for teachers to collaborate are part of your direct instructional leadership of your staff. Teachers might need help learning how to better design and analyze results from the type of assessments they have always conducted or how to quickly and efficiently conduct periodic assessments of individual students. Grade-level groups may meet together to discuss assessment results, often selecting a few children as the focus. They may discuss instructional strategies to better meet the needs of these children or ways to regroup them for skills-based instruction. These activities are, and have historically been, basic professional expectations of general education teachers. They also duplicate the expectations of Tier 1 of RTI.

You will also act as a bridge between your school and the district when it comes to implementing more intensive supports, whether or not you incorporate the term *RTI* in describing them.

Review the approaches your school uses to support struggling students. Since school resources, staff time, and student time are limited, implement programs that are most likely to provide effective extra help to students with skill gaps that might hamper their forward progress.

Remember to celebrate the incremental steps of progress made by struggling learners with the same degree of enthusiasm you show for those who meet proficiency and help the school make AYP. As principal, you are responsible for ensuring that all students are valued and that every child receives the school's best effort to help him or her move forward to the next skill level. Students are motivated by evidence of their own success, and teachers are motivated by evidence they have made a positive difference. You will find that your own morale is bolstered by this evidence as well.

Assessment Framework Template

	Summative	Benchmark	Formative
Gr. 6			
Gr. 5			
Gr. 4			
Gr. 3			
Gr. 2			
Gr. 1			
K			
PreK			

5

Data to Strengthen Classroom Instruction

The use of data to guide schoolwide decision making and to deliver support for struggling students is complex, challenging, and critical—but not sufficient. As illustrated earlier in figure 1.1 (page 9), the principal's influence extends to a wide range of staff groups and individual teachers. The most direct impact on student learning is in the classroom with the relationships teachers develop with students and the instructional skills they employ. This most intimate of instructional settings is sometimes perceived as the teacher's personal territory, and the principal's influence demands both human relations skills to build professional trust and pedagogical skills to recognize and develop excellent instruction.

Principals' Roles With Teachers

The principal interacts with staff members in various settings and groups for many purposes. Strengthening classroom instruction requires aligning the use of data with the positional leadership roles of the principal, which include responsibilities for evaluation, supervision, and professional development.

Evaluation

Teacher evaluation is the most formal interaction between principal and staff, and it is the most prescribed by way of contract language and legal precedent. It typically occurs for a subset of the staff each year, on a cyclical basis. Most teacher-evaluation processes require a set of classroom visits, preceded by some communication about the planned instruction and followed by a conference and written summary. The summative evaluation may suggest goals, but it is, by and large, a statement of whether the teacher's performance is satisfactory to continue.

Whether and how data on student learning become linked to teacher evaluation is being played out in some states at the time of this writing. Linking student learning to teacher performance fairly and accurately will require precision and patience. As Sawchuk (2011) points out:

> The debate about "value-added" measures of teaching may be the most divisive topic in teacher-quality policy today. It has generated sharp-tongued exchanges in public forums, in news stories, and on editorial pages. And it has produced enough policy briefs to fell whole forests. But for most of the nation's teachers, who do not teach subjects or grades in which value-added data are available, that debate is largely irrelevant. (p. 1)

Various estimates place the percentage of teachers for whom no pre- and post-measures of student growth are available as high as 70 percent. Legitimate concerns must be addressed about the best type of student assessment in various disciplines; about how to make assessments comparable across schools, districts, and states; about how to account for differences in student populations; and more. At the time of this writing, only a dozen or so states have passed legislation requiring that evidence of students' academic growth be included in teacher evaluation systems. Readers are advised to watch developments in New York, Rhode Island, Tennessee, North Carolina, and Colorado as they take first steps in this direction. Helpful websites include the Center for American Progress (www.americanprogress.org) and the National Comprehensive Center for Teacher Quality (www.tqsource.org).

Meanwhile, principals will continue to conduct teacher evaluations according to existing policies and procedures. Although that is a formal role of the principal that must be fulfilled, it is not the focus of this chapter. In most settings, some time will pass before student learning data are included in the summative decision about whether a teacher is satisfactory to continue employment. That does not excuse avoidance of using the data to strengthen classroom instruction through the supervisory role of the principal, as discussed later in the "Feedback and Performance Improvement" section of this chapter.

Supervision

The distinction between summative and formative assessment of student learning helps clarify the difference between evaluation and supervision in the roles of the principal. The conversations and visits that are part of the formal evaluation process are quite clearly labeled as such, so other interactions between principal and staff are recognized as "not evaluation" and may be more comfortable and natural—but the principal is never *not* the supervisor. The principal may say, "This is just a casual comment," or "This is just informal," or "This is just social," but even if the principal thinks he has left his supervisor hat back in the office, teachers still see it hovering above his head.

This chapter focuses on uses of both teaching and learning data in order to strengthen classroom instruction throughout the routines and in explicit activities of the school day and year. Every aspect of this chapter would fall under the heading Instructional Leadership.

Professional Development and Support

Leadership involves diagnosing and influencing what happens throughout the school. It includes holding people accountable for high performance. On the flip side of the coin, it includes ensuring that people have the knowledge, skills, and capacity to do what is expected. Providing professional development and support for staff is the principal role that mostly closely mirrors classroom teaching for students.

Chapter 2 introduced four categories of data that should be part of the information used in decisions. One of these was staff-related data. The use of data related to teacher education and experience is *not* for the purpose of evaluation but for the purpose of planning. Professional development to strengthen the quality of instruction can take one of two directions. It can be designed on the assumption that everybody needs the *same* thing and "one size fits all" will work just fine—which too often has been the case. The alternative is to plan professional development based on an assumption that everybody can improve but people have different needs—in which case you must have information about what the needs are.

The National Staff Development Council (formerly NSDC; renamed Learning Forward) is actually international and the premier organization focused directly on building teacher capacity and the improvement of instruction. As Executive Director Stephanie Hirsh (2009) states: "NSDC's theory of change stands on the assumption that students achieve more when teams of educators within a school and across a district engage in continuous cycles of improvement that focus their attention on their learning needs, as defined by student learning needs, refining their practice and accessing district and external assistance providers to support their efforts" (p. 5). Since student learning needs are not all the same, teacher learning needs are not going to be all the same or at the same time, so it becomes abundantly clear that "one size fits all" professional development is not only insulting, it is a poor use of scarce resources that should be more strategically directed.

Four aspects of professional development should be differentiated: what, how much, what kind, and where and when. The topics (*what*) of professional development will change as student-performance data identify skills of greatest need and teacher-preparation data identify gaps in education and experience to meet the student needs. Some teachers are already experts and don't need more individual or initial training. Their development would focus on building capacity to develop skill in others. The amount or degree of professional development (*how much*) varies by experiential factors, such as how long it has been, if ever, since a teacher taught that content and how much the academic rigor of the relevant standards may have changed in the meantime. The type or level (*what kind*) of professional development needed depends on whether the knowledge or skill is brand new and the teacher needs to start with the introductory theory, research, and examples or whether the concepts are familiar and it is time to engage in practice with feedback through peer observation or coaching. Decisions about the most effective setting and timing (*where* and *when*) emerge once the need and goal have been established through the earlier discussions.

This is a quantum leap from the traditional practice of identifying this year's new thing, sitting everyone down for three hours on the first day back from summer vacation, baptizing them in the perspiration of a hot gymnasium, and anointing them to "go forth and implement." But differentiating in so many directions (what, how much, what kind, where and when) would require leaders to have either blind faith that all teachers will choose what they really need or diagnostic information to guide choices and to collaboratively develop goal-oriented individual and team plans. After using student performance data to identify *their* greatest learning needs, the data on *teachers'* related learning needs would include self-assessment, peer assessment, and student assessment.

What Data Are You Looking For?

The principal should look for background information that provides knowledge of teachers' training and experience as well as data about current practice. Four types of data that help determine the effectiveness of instruction in a school are discussed here. Although terminology and priorities vary from district to district and state to state, few would argue that principals need to see (1) instruction linked to academic standards, (2) students actively engaged in their classes, (3) teachers using instructional practices that have been linked to increased learning, and (4) evidence that agreed-upon school improvement strategies are being implemented.

Evidence of Teaching to Standards

In today's standards-based educational environment, both principals and teachers need a clear understanding of what students are expected to know and be able to do. Marshall (2003) states:

> When a principal visits a classroom, one of the most important things to look for is whether the teacher is on target with the curriculum. Of course, to answer the question means that the principal must know what exactly the curriculum is. . . . Teacher supervision can't be efficient and effective until curriculum expectations are clear and widely accepted within the school. (p. 705)

Many districts have worked to develop curriculum guides that are carefully aligned with their standards. These curriculum guides and the related pacing guides provide road maps for elements of instruction that principals should observe while in classrooms. These road maps are especially helpful when visiting the classroom of a teacher whose students are demonstrating less progress than those of another teacher working at the same grade level or teaching the same content. If your teachers have pacing guides available to them, familiarize yourself with the content that should be taught during the general time period of your visit. Do you see a lesson that focuses on teaching this content? If not, talk with the teacher about the reasons why. Is he or she having difficulty keeping students' progress on track? If so, some assistance for the teacher—or for students experiencing difficulty—might be needed. Your follow-up support might focus on providing opportunities for the teacher to observe in another classroom, or perhaps the grade-level teachers could meet together to discuss ways to better support low-performing students.

Evidence of Student Engagement

Every principal has gone into classrooms that are vibrant examples of students engaged in learning and into classrooms in which students' attention is wandering. Does the teacher make use of a variety of approaches—whole class as well as small group? Does he intentionally encourage responses from all students? Are students given time to process chunks of information with their peers so they rehearse and restate what they have learned?

Learning can be standards-based and also fun, but student engagement is about more than enjoyment and reducing misbehavior. Researchers like Marzano (2007) and others have substantiated the academic benefits of physical activity, social processing, and other strategies that create a highly engaged classroom.

Evidence of Instructional Strategies

A positive benefit of the educational reform emphasis on research-based programs and practices is that schools and districts have much easier access to resources that validate powerful instructional strategies and that offer training and coaching. Expected practices may be found in evaluation documents, in district policy, and in systemwide professional development initiatives.

The example in figure 5.1 (page 72) is referred to as a *teacher evaluation rubric*, but it need not be used in that way. It provides a snapshot of how a continuum of characteristics can facilitate discussion with individuals and small groups. The principal must possess knowledge and understanding of the instructional strategies that have been identified as expectations and that have been taught and coached with teachers so that he or she can recognize them accurately, reinforce their effective use, and provide feedback and support where these strategies are not present or are used inappropriately. For example, the strategy of formative assessment presents a two-fold challenge: (1) to acquire or develop good formative assessments that align with the local curriculum, and (2) to ensure these assessments are *used* in formative ways. *Formativeness* is not just a function of how long or short the instrument is or how often it is given. Formative use of assessment information means that the teacher uses it to understand how students are *form*ing new concepts and skills, to in*form* instructional plans for the following day/week, and to *form* flexible groups for additional help. Instructional coaches and other teacher leaders play valuable roles, but the bottom-line responsibility for ensuring strong classroom instruction is painted across the threshold of the principal's door.

Evidence of Schoolwide Implementation

If the district has recommended or mandated a set of research-validated instructional strategies, the school improvement plan should refer to using them as one of the strategies for addressing student learning needs. If no such district decision has been made, the school improvement/leadership team should have identified some strategies for focus in classrooms. Those teaching practices represent the overlap between evidence of instructional strategies and evidence of strategy implementation.

School improvement plans usually include other kinds of strategies as well. For example, chapter 4 referred to differentiation and to providing schoolwide systems of support such as RTI. Plans may also address uses of new technology such as interactive whiteboards or programs to address affective areas such as bullying prevention. In addition, the plan needs a set of indicators of implementation (see chapter 3) that provide evidence of these practices and programs being used consistently and as intended. Gathering these data is also part of the principal's role in strengthening classroom instruction.

The Teacher:

4 = The Expert	3 = Proficient	2 = Needs Improvement	1 = Does Not Meet Standards
Posts the criteria for proficient work, including rubrics and exemplars, and students internalize them	Posts clear criteria for proficiency, including rubrics and exemplars of student work	Tells students some of the qualities that their finished work should exhibit	Expects students to know (or figure out) what it takes to get good grades
Uses a variety of first-rate assessments to diagnose and continuously monitor students' learning	Diagnoses students' knowledge and skills up front and uses a variety of assessments during each unit	Uses pencil-and-paper quizzes and tests with some open-ended questions to assess student learning	Uses only multiple-choice and short-answer pencil-and-paper tests to assess student learning
Continuously checks for understanding, unscrambles confusion, and gives specific, helpful feedback	Frequently checks for understanding and gives students helpful feedback if they seem confused	Asks questions to determine whether students understand	Rarely takes time to check for understanding
Has students set ambitious goals, self-assess and monitor, and take responsibility for their progress	Has students set goals, self-assess, and know where they stand academically at all times	Urges students to look over their tests, see where they had trouble, and aim to improve those areas	Urges students to work harder and be more careful on future tests
Frequently posts students' work with rubrics and commentary and uses it to motivate and direct effort	Regularly posts students' work to make visible and celebrate their progress with respect to standards	Posts some A student work as an example for others	Posts only a few samples of A work
Immediately uses interim assessment data to fine-tune teaching, reteach, and help struggling students	Uses data from interim assessments to adjust teaching, reteach, and follow up with failing students	Looks over students' tests to determine whether anything needs to be retaught	Looks over unit and final tests to identify any lessons for the future
Relentlessly follows up with struggling students using time and support to reach proficiency	Takes responsibility for students who are not succeeding and tenaciously gives them extra help	Offers students who fail tests additional time to study and do retakes	Tells students that if they fail a test, that's it; the class has to move on to cover the curriculum
Makes sure students who need specialized diagnosis and help receive appropriate services on a timely basis	When necessary, refers students for specialized diagnosis and extra help	Sometimes doesn't refer students promptly for special help or refers students who don't need it	Either fails to refer students for special education or refers students who do not need it
Charts and analyzes assessment data, draws action conclusions, and shares them with others	Analyzes data from summative assessments, draws conclusions, and shares them appropriately	Records students' grades and notices some general patterns for future reference	Records students' grades and moves on with the curriculum
Constantly reflects on the effectiveness of teaching strategies, lessons, and units and works daily to improve them	Reflects on the effectiveness of lessons and units and continuously works to improve them	At the end of a teaching unit or semester, thinks about what might have been done better	When a teaching unit or lesson doesn't go well, chalks it up to experience

Source: Reprinted with permission from Marshall (2006b).

Figure 5.1: A continuum of teaching behaviors.

How Will You Find the Data?

Data to strengthen classroom instruction can come from a variety of sources. An obvious source of data, referred to earlier in this chapter, is the typical supervisory practice of informal observations in classrooms. Another way to gather data in a more focused manner is through the use of a customized walkthrough tool. While only the principal can do teacher evaluations, the principal is not the only one who can gather data about classroom practice. Teachers can generate additional information through self- and peer observations and through collaborative analysis of student work. Individual conversations with staff members can also create a private venue for discussion of student learning and should not be neglected.

Teacher Observation

Ensuring that quality teaching occurs in every classroom is among a principal's most important responsibilities. Student performance on required end-of-the-year assessments provides one source of data about the quality of instruction, but waiting until the end of the year might mean many months of missed opportunities to help teachers improve their instructional skills. The annual checklist observations of teachers used by many districts for evaluation purposes also suffer from the "too little, too late" problem.

More frequent and targeted classroom visits, on the other hand, can yield valuable information about what happens in classrooms on a day-to-day basis. When followed up with feedback to and conversations with teachers, it provides principals with a powerful tool for improving instruction. Williams, Cray, Millen, and Protheroe (2002) view teacher observations as

> an essential means of enhancing the professional knowledge and skills of teachers and building their confidence to meet the needs of diverse learners. Rather than single, isolated events, teacher observations should be a regular part of the professional working environment, seamlessly integrated with the overall professional development process. (p. 14)

The framework in table 5.1 (page 74) contrasts traditional and new paradigms of teacher observations and suggests that the new paradigm better addresses today's "challenges of creating and sustaining a high-performing teaching and learning environment" (p. 18).

While principals should routinely dedicate time to make and journal classroom observations, visits can also serve other specific purposes, such as:

- Intervening to rectify a problem, when expectations for instruction or the appropriate treatment of students are not being met

- Coaching to improve, when the teacher is working to refine a specific practice or to deal more effectively with a particular situation

- Monitoring the implementation of a program or component of a model to ensure that the program is being implemented as intended (fidelity)

- Responding to a teacher's request for assistance in handling a particular situation, and seeking suggestions for learning strategies to achieve a specific learning goal or working with a particular type of student

- Affirming and reinforcing the teacher's growth, effectiveness, or success in implementing a new practice

- Documenting and recording specific techniques or examples of student learning. (Williams et al., 2002, p. 26–27)

Table 5.1: Paradigms for Teacher Observation

Traditional Paradigm	New Paradigm
Infrequent and brief classroom observations	Frequent observations of varied lessons or practices
Focus on student behavior	Focus on student learning
Focus on classroom management	Focus on effective teaching
Judgments based on personal philosophy and teaching style	Judgments based on research-based pedagogy
Focus on lesson plans	Focus on student learning and engagement
Focus on curriculum standards and learning objectives	Focus on evidence of student learning
"One size fits all" observations	Contextually appropriate observations
Single observation method and protocol	Multiple observation methods and protocols
Changes in practice based on principal recommendations	Changes in practice based on professional development goals and plans
Each observation a discrete event	Observations part of a teacher development process linked to goals and prior observation results
Feedback from principal only	Feedback connected to collaborative dialogue with other teachers

Source: Adapted from Williams et al., 2002, p. 19.

Customized Walkthroughs

The customized walkthrough provides a specific focus that is most directly linked to the purpose of monitoring a program or model to ensure it is being implemented as intended. Chapter 3 described a four-step process for ensuring that implementation occurs, which included identifying indicators of implementation and designing tools and a process for gathering evidence that would generate desired statements of results. The criteria on a customized walkthrough form could also include specific instructional strategies that staff are focusing on during a given period of time.

For example, from a range of models and sources, a school chose five elements of powerful teaching on which to focus during the entire year (Holcomb, 2007). These included:

- High expectations, clearly stated and consistently enforced

- Important curricular content, relevant and standards-based

- Student-centered lessons with active participation

- Challenging material, high on the taxonomy

- Frequent assessment and feedback

A simple walkthrough form was created with a column for each of these teaching behaviors. The principal set a goal of spending at least one hour a day, three days of each week, to do ten drop-in visits. Generous credit was given for any indication of a positive teaching behavior, which was recorded with a check. At every faculty meeting, it was easy for the principal to provide group feedback such as the number of walkthroughs and the percentage of time each behavior was in evidence. Over the course of a year, all the teaching elements increased, but frequent assessment and feedback remained consistently the lowest. Based on that data, professional development for the next year focused on formative assessment.

Self and Peer Observation

The principal has a responsibility to be in classrooms on a regular basis and to use a focused method of note-taking or record keeping so feedback can be provided. But the principal cannot do it all, and the research on shared leadership stresses the importance of teacher leadership. The need for opportunities to collaborate has been stressed in previous chapters of this book and is reemphasized here. As Shirley (2009) reminds us, "innovative leaders provide teachers with opportunities to observe other teachers so they can develop other frames of reference on their teaching. When they are given these opportunities, even excellent teachers report they find valuable new ideas for diversifying their instructional repertoire" (p. 145).

Teachers need mirrors to be able to gain an accurate picture of their practice. An inexpensive video camera can provide opportunities for teachers to observe themselves in action. For some, this will be less threatening because no one else needs to see the video. For many, it will provide both reinforcement and surprises. For the most hesitant, the camera can be aimed toward the class rather than the teacher. Watching what students are doing during instruction can also provide valuable and surprising information.

A more courageous step for the teacher is to identify one or two colleagues and ask them to view the video or a selected segment and to then provide reactions and suggestions. The teacher may also identify a need from watching his or her own video and then ask to observe a colleague teaching that skill or dealing with that kind of challenge.

A blend of principal observation and peer observation occurred in the example of a principal who was concerned about the amount of whole-class, teacher-directed instruction he was seeing during his classroom visits. He decided to include teachers in the observation process. Time that had been set aside for professional development was reallocated to teachers doing "multiple pop-in visits to as many classrooms as they could reasonably visit in one class period" (McEnery, 2005, p. 45). Teachers were asked to use an observation form provided by the principal to record what they observed teachers and students doing. After pulling together and sharing data from these multiple observations, the principal provided time for teachers to discuss their observations. In the principal's view, the observations and the resulting discussions provided motivation for change with teachers asking for professional development focused on use of less teacher-directed strategies.

Collaborative Analysis of Student Work

Through peer observations, teachers can see each other in action. Another way of using data to strengthen classroom instruction is to look at the effects of the teaching as it is reflected in student work. Gregory and Kuzmich (2004) point out that "colleagues sitting down to look at and discuss student work . . . are practicing an essential form of assessment data collection" (p. 69).

This section includes several step-by-step protocols for collaborative analysis of student work. A more gentle, general approach would be to choose *just two or three* of the following questions as prompts for informal teacher discussion:

- Here's what I see as the strengths of my class. How about you?

- Here's what I see as the needs of my students. How about you? Needs as a whole class? Needs for small groups? Needs as individual students?

- What instruction needs to occur to move my class (our students) ahead? As a whole? As small groups? For individual students?

- What patterns are we noticing?

- What commonalities do we see within a class? Our grade level? The whole school?

- What goals can I set for particular students? For the class? For myself?

- What can I do to impact those patterns? Do any lessons need to be eliminated? Do any lessons need to be added?

- How will reteaching be different from the first time I taught it?

- It looks like your students did really well. What did you do (differently) that helped your students succeed where my students may not have done so well?

- What can I learn from my colleagues?

- What interventions or enrichments are needed, and how will those supports stay connected to classroom instruction?

- What types of intervention and enrichment activities could we provide for our students within the regular classroom setting?

- Discuss use of the assessment. What went well? What was most useful? Are there things we need to revisit about the assessment?

- What teacher learning do I need to make this learning happen for my students? Teacher support? Teaching resources?

- What specific steps will we take to offer these specific students [names] help with this specific skill [most essential benchmark]?

For constructed responses, essays, and reports, Gregory and Kuzmich (2007) propose that collaborative analysis includes questions that focus teachers on higher-level thinking, such as: What was the level of critical thinking students demonstrated? Did it match the standards? Did the prompt and scoring guide clearly push students to higher levels? Did students receive instruction and learning activities at this level of rigor prior to the assessment? Other helpful techniques include guidelines for looking at student work, the tuning protocol, the collaborative goals protocol, and time for collaborative analysis.

Guidelines for Looking at Student Work

The following guidelines were developed by the Philadelphia Education Fund based on the work of a variety of education organizations and practitioners. The purpose is to help teacher teams get started with a process of inquiry.

1. Gather a team, or small group, of teachers together.

2. Select a piece of student work. The sample should demonstrate a rich variety of student learning. It can be a work in progress, a final piece, or a document of a performance. Also collect the scoring guide or rubric used to assess that piece. Make copies for team members, if possible.

3. If someone in the group is not familiar with your unit of study, take a few minutes to introduce its overall purpose, the activities that have been conducted, and the work that has been generated.

4. Discuss and write down one standard that you expected students to address in this activity. What did you expect the students to know and be able to do?

5. Next, take a few minutes to look at the work as a group. Either read it aloud or let each person take a turn looking at it.

6. Write down the group's observations about the work. Then write down comments and questions. You might allow each team member to do this first individually and then share in turn.

7. Next, use your scoring guide or rubric to assess the piece of work. If you do not yet have a scoring guide, reread the standard you have identified and assess the work based on its criteria.

8. Take a few minutes to discuss as a team the following questions: What can you see from your observations, comments, and questions that will help you assess student learning? How might these observations determine your next steps as a teacher? Do these observations tell you anything new about your unit of study or classroom activities? (Philadelphia Education Fund, n.d.).

Another approach to collaboration around student work samples is the tuning protocol, created by the Coalition of Essential Schools.

The Tuning Protocol

This structured, facilitated conversation involves a group of teachers (and sometimes others) examining samples of student work to address a focusing question—usually about instructional practice or the quality of student work. The tuning protocol is often used as a way to address questions related to the goals or standards for an individual classroom or school.

A typical tuning protocol brings together a small group of teachers (ten to fifteen) with a facilitator who may come from outside or inside the school. One teacher (or a team of teachers) presents sample student work and the context for the work (the assignment or assessment rubric). The protocol follows a schedule calling for presentation of the task or project, clarifying questions, examination of student work samples, providing "warm" (supportive) and "cool" (challenging) feedback to presenting teachers, reflection by the presenting teacher, and debriefing of the process. The entire protocol takes about an hour and fifteen minutes.

This protocol may be used as a one-shot instrument for addressing an important schoolwide question or issue or as part of ongoing professional development or planning. The tuning protocol can be modified and adjusted for use in the classroom as a peer review and exhibition tool.

Classroom Goals Protocol

One district provided time for teachers to talk about student work using a more detailed process on an ongoing basis. Teachers in all schools met one day a month to evaluate results from a range of student assessments and to plan instruction based on the results. Principals created teams of three to four teachers, with each of the teams working together for the entire school year. The classroom goals protocol was developed by district staff developers and pilot teams of teachers to guide their work.

Prior to each month's meeting, each teacher prepares by selecting an area in which students are struggling. The teacher collects student work, either a formative or common summative assessment that demonstrates where students are having difficulty. The teacher then uses the protocol's forms to prepare a brief analysis of students' performance and to outline the lesson focus and assessment task for background to share with the team. In addition to the completed form, teachers bring six samples of student work, representing two high-scoring students, two average-scoring students, and two low-scoring students.

During the meeting, the team focuses on three questions:

1. Did your assessment match your instructional strategies?

2. What were student strengths?

3. What were student weaknesses? (Johnston, Knight, & Miller, 2007, p. 16)

During discussion, other teachers on the team suggest instructional strategies intended to address the area of concern. The teacher tries some of the suggested strategies, gathers data related to their impact, and returns to the group for more discussion the next month. The small size of the teams provides time for each of its members to discuss issues in depth.

In addition to these monthly classroom-goals meetings, other teams in the elementary schools met weekly to focus on: (1) curriculum planning and classroom assessment and (2) student interventions. Most elementary principals provide the time for these weekly forty-minute sessions by having teachers work together for thirty minutes before students arrive and then continuing for another ten to fourteen minutes while other staff members—such as the literacy coach—lead short learning activities for students (Johnston et al., 2007).

Time for Collaborative Analysis

Time is one of the critical issues in empowering teachers to examine student work together. Hord and Sommers (2008) provide a substantial list of suggestions on how districts and schools can provide time for this teacher collaboration:

- Have a longer school day four days per week; use time "saved" on another day (the fifth) for professionals to meet, study, plan.

- Extend each day of the week by ten minutes for an early or late start to provide a periodic release day.

- Extend the school day a half hour on Monday, Tuesday, Thursday, and Friday; on Wednesday, staff are involved in professional development and dialogue from 8:00–10:30 a.m. Students arrive at 10:30 a.m. for a modified day of thematic work, community activities, and so on.

- Bank time by choosing one hour per week before or after school in study groups—compensated by districtwide professional development days.

- Consider the possibility of gaining time from how lunch periods are scheduled.

- Add minutes to the beginning and end of four days; give a half day off to students on the fifth day.

- Cut down on passing time to build time available for teachers to meet.

- "School day" becomes "school week," with beginning and ending hours of each day flexible for schools.

- Extend to eight-hour paid workday for teachers, principals, and all others who directly support learning.

- Extend school year to gain days.

- Teams choose a day to come in an hour early or stay an hour late and document attendance and accomplishments; in exchange, staff do not have to come on district planning days.

- Meet after school or on Saturday, and document it as the professional development hours in contract.

- Meet beyond the "contract" day in exchange for being able to leave early on another day.

- Seek waivers from state for instructional contact hours.

- Reconsider the use of scheduled faculty meetings.

- Teachers from one grade level invite students in for "buddy work" with older students while the other grade-level teachers meet; exchange the trade another day.

- Use professional development money in grants to hire floating subs that release one grade level/department at a time during the day.

Schools and districts find that increasing the time and opportunities teachers have to review and discuss student work together can have a positive impact on efforts to strengthen instruction.

Individual Conversations

Although principals often talk with teachers *after* having been in their classrooms, the value of conversations for their own sake should not be overlooked. Individual conversations can be a proactive and intentional strategy for gathering information about instruction and especially about what teachers perceive as their strengths and needs. When the *principal* is new, individual conversations serve the dual purpose of building relationships and gathering perceptual data about classroom instruction and teacher needs.

When *teachers* are new, individual conversations are also critical because the newcomers may not feel comfortable or confident to speak up in teacher groups or to approach the principal and initiate a one-on-one conversation. Ask new teachers how things are going. Find out what they consider particularly helpful in providing them with support as well as what they see as barriers. Then use these data to identify ways you and the rest of the staff can better support them.

Encourage new teachers to assess their own use of instructional strategies by paying special attention to a few students. Suggest they reflect on questions such as: Are these students engaged? Have they all demonstrated understanding of instructions and assignments? Do any lessons seem to go especially well for them—or not so well? Spending time with a new teacher to structure these reflections and to then discuss what they learned can help improve instruction while beginning the development of data analysis skills.

How Will You Use the Data?

The principal is now loaded with data about classroom instruction. He or she has the summaries of key findings direct from the schoolwide analysis of student learning data. He or she may have survey information that was compiled during the assembling of the school portfolio. Now he can add quantifiable data from the use of walkthrough forms and anecdotal data from journaling his classroom observations and conversations with teachers. Meeting notes from groups of teachers who looked at student work together may also be at the principal's disposal.

Similar to the way that schoolwide decision making included both celebrations and concerns, principal decision making about how to strengthen classroom instruction needs to be based on both areas of strength and areas for growth. Just as the teacher needs skill-specific and student-specific data to provide individual interventions and group students with common needs, the principal needs to summarize information about individual teachers and groups so he or she can use the data for feedback, professional development planning, and providing support.

Feedback and Performance Improvement

If, as a principal, you have ever looked out the window and wondered why the superintendent's car is pulling into the visitor space, you can understand how teachers react when their boss steps into the classroom—no matter how much a part of the principal's routine practice it is. The teacher's first thought is, "What does she want?" Then, as the principal leaves the room, the teacher's thought is, "What did she think?" Adults need frequent, specific, timely feedback just as much as students do in order to learn and grow.

Kaplan and Owings (2001) provide guidelines for principals who are reviewing their approach to teacher observation and follow-up:

- Make teaching effectiveness and working closely with teachers in classroom observations and conferencing a priority.

- Vigorously seek instructional best practices in all classroom observations and teacher conferences.

- Visit all classrooms frequently for at least ten minutes and look for instructional best practices even when they are not part of a formal summative assessment.

- Give teachers specific, positive feedback about what you observed.

Short, written feedback can be as simple as a sticky note left on the classroom door, emphasizing a positive you observed. Verbal follow-ups can take place during brief, stand-up conversations in the corridor or elsewhere the two interact during the course of the day. The principal can summarize perceptions in a brief three- to five-minute chat and either conclude the exchange or reveal the need for a more extended conversation.

Data related to common schoolwide efforts such as improving behavior management, focusing on specific instructional strategies, or implementing other initiatives in the school improvement plan should be provided as feedback to the staff as a whole. An example of this was provided earlier in this chapter, when the principal shared walkthrough data at each faculty meeting.

The primary purposes of individual and group feedback are to reinforce expectations, reward effort, and sustain motivation. Teachers who are doing well feel commended and can volunteer to help others. Teachers who are struggling can be provided with professional development and support. Teachers who aren't trying yet will be indirectly reminded that they are not contributing or supporting their colleagues.

There may be times when the indirect reminders of expectations embedded in data discussions do not stimulate action on the part of a staff member, and the principal will have to move from providing feedback to the whole staff or a teacher team to providing individual feedback of a sterner nature. Unwillingness of a teacher to examine and use data about his or her student learning must be confronted. Failure to adopt new practices that have been identified as schoolwide commitments must be addressed. The principal should initiate an individual conversation, which can begin with the observation, "As I work with the entire staff to help us all move forward, I am afraid I may be missing something, and I don't want to draw any erroneous conclusions from that. I haven't been able to see [name the desired practice] in evidence in your classroom or in your comments, and I want to open this conversation so you can share your thoughts with me. Please talk with me about what you've been trying and what you've run into." This approach serves notice that you expect evidence but gives the staff member the first opportunity to fill in any blanks (no principal can see everything) and acknowledges that it's OK to run into difficulty with something new. Depending on the teacher's response, the principal may identify professional development needs or other supports to provide for the teacher. In a few cases, the response may actually be resistance or refusal, which then moves the principal's role to a more authoritative approach, such as a professional-improvement goal developed jointly or, if necessary, a plan of improvement developed through the formal evaluation process.

Professional Development

Translating the data into opportunities for teacher development is an ethical responsibility that can yield substantial benefits, making it well worth the effort. By forging a strong and clear link between teacher observation and teacher development, you take an important step toward the goal of ensuring a high-performing teacher in every classroom. The purpose is to "identify a teacher's current levels of knowledge and skill and use them as the basis for a coherent and documented plan for that teacher's continued learning and professional development" (Holland, 2005, p. 72).

When the evidence about teacher practice and/or student learning raises concerns, possible causes need to be considered. For example, if the teacher joined the staff *after* that wonderful initial training, he needs to be able to access it some other way. If the teacher has changed grade levels or schools, she may lack content knowledge or familiarity with the curriculum. The principal must use the data about teaching and learning to identify underlying needs for schoolwide professional development, common needs for small-group learning through avenues such as webinars and book-study groups, and unique needs to be clarified through individual conversations. Hirsh (2011) points out the need for a balance of schoolwide, group, and individual professional development, stressing that:

> Targeted professional development doesn't erase the continued need for team and schoolwide professional learning in which educators examine data for grade levels, subject areas, or entire schools; set achievement goals for larger groups of students; and engage in professional learning to meet those goals. Through these collaborative professional learning opportunities, teachers develop collective responsibility for ensuring that all students have access to the best teaching. (p. 5)

Support

Marshall (2006b) points out that the "kindest thing a principal can do for an underperforming teacher is to give candid, evidence-based feedback and robust follow-up support" (p. 1). Supports may include resource materials, peers who can serve as coaches or who themselves can be observed, professional development programs, courses, or independent study options.

As Louis et al. (2010) point out, "Supportive interaction among teachers . . . enables them to assume various roles with one another as mentor, mentee, coach, specialist, advisor, facilitator, and so on" (p. 44). In some cases, especially those in which a teacher has a unique assignment shared with no one else in the school, the support will need to come from a colleague with the same role in another school or through the central office, university, or intermediate service agency.

Your Role as Principal

Research is providing an increasingly strong base of information—written in practitioner-relevant language—about good teaching strategies. The first role of the principal is to constantly cultivate a solid foundation of knowledge about good teaching. Have you been an active participant in the professional development provided to teachers so you share the common language and focus and can speak with credibility?

Many educators are recognizing the role that effective teacher-observation can play in helping teachers continually grow and improve their performance. Stansbury (2001) suggests that teacher observation should be embedded in the day-to-day work of professional growth and classroom practice. As principal, you should ask yourself, "Is the approach I am using for teacher observation, or one I am thinking about using, designed to help teachers strengthen their abilities to teach all students to high standards?"

The National Association of Elementary School Principals (NAESP; 2001) recognizes the importance of using data to strengthen classroom instruction:

> Effective principals spend large amounts of time in classrooms, observing the teaching of academic units and provide detailed feedback regarding how teachers' effectiveness can be improved. The point of principal and peer observations is not to catch a teacher doing something wrong. The point is to ensure that all students are meaningfully engaged, actively learning, and that teachers are not simply presenting material. An important part of classroom observations is to . . . assist teachers in improving those skills and to help them grow professionally. Collaboration with other teachers and assignment of a mentor may be strategies a principal suggests to assist the teacher, but the conversation often begins between principal and teacher. School leaders support teachers' professionalism by sharing feedback with teachers about objectives of lessons, the degree of student engagement and the behavior of students. (p. 33)

Reflection on your role in strengthening classroom instruction will include the following questions. Use the reproducible on page 85, Reflections on How I Strengthen Classroom Instruction, to record your reflections.

- How often am I in classrooms? What evidence do I see of good teaching and high levels of learning?

- What kinds of feedback do I share with teachers after observing their classes? Does this feedback focus on the teacher's lessons, methods of instruction, and student learning? Does it focus on the extent to which all students were engaged in meaningful and relevant instructional activities?

- How do I engage teachers in individual and small-group discussions of their students' results on formative and large-scale assessments? Am I sure that less successful teachers realize their students are not doing as well? Meyers and Rust (2000) stress the importance of helping teachers learn how to "assess their own work and its impact on their students" (p. 34). To be successful, school leaders need to engage in conversations with teachers, using assessment data to diagnose strengths as well as areas in which the teachers need to modify their instruction. In addition, by providing teachers with time and opportunity for discussion that uses assessment data as a springboard, principals can strengthen a school's instructional program.

- How do I use what I learn from students and student work to help teachers improve their practice?

- Do I know my staff well enough to recognize how their backgrounds may lead to differences in ability and approach? According to Williams et al. (2002), "accepting diversity in a staff means recognizing that teachers differ in their ability to examine their own practices and in their openness to having others examine their work. They also differ in the readiness, knowledge, skills, and orientations they bring to the teaching and learning process. Principals must approach their role with the same appreciation for teacher diversity that they expect teachers to recognize in their students" (pp. 11–12).

As you engage with data on classroom instruction and encourage teachers to examine the bottom line of evidence of student learning, remember that it can feel uncomfortable even to the most professional teacher because it's new and different. It can feel downright terrifying to the teacher who knows it may reveal shortcomings. Practice the golden rule for data: *Data unto others as you would have them data unto you.*

Reflections on How I Strengthen Classroom Instruction

How often am I in classrooms? What are the barriers that interfere? How can I rearrange my priorities during the school day?	
What evidence do I see of good teaching and high levels of learning? How do I reinforce this?	
What kinds of feedback do I share with teachers after informal observations and classroom visits?	
How do I keep data so that I can aggregate what I see and share it with all staff to reinforce and increase practice?	
Does my feedback focus on the teacher's methods of instruction—aligned with a common instructional framework?	
To what degree does my feedback focus on the extent of student talk and action?	
To what degree does my feedback focus on evidence that learning is occurring? Did occur?	
How do I engage teachers in individual and small group discussions of their students' results on formative and large-scale assessments?	
How sure am I that less successful teachers realize their students are not doing as well?	
How do I use what I learn from students and student work to help teachers improve their practice?	
Do I know my staff well enough to recognize how their backgrounds may lead to differences in ability and approach? How do I use this understanding to shape the way I supervise and support them?	

6

Data for Principal Planning and Performance

The case has been made for data-based decision making as an essential skill and role of the principal. Several schoolwide decision-making functions overlap with district policy and practice within which principals must work while advocating for changes that empower new practices on behalf of students in the school. The most powerful school factor on student learning is, of course, the relationships and instructional practices that occur in the classroom. Based on data the principal acquires about student learning and teaching expertise, he or she must provide feedback, target professional development to match needs, and support and guide individual and group efforts. In this chapter, the principal will analyze these data to plan, set goals, and improve his or her own performance.

What Data Are You Looking For?

As principal, you will need to use all the data described in the preceding chapters, for all the purposes outlined, plus more—and less. It is, indeed, a daunting challenge but one with very rewarding potential benefits and three reassuring realities.

First, "doing all the things already described here" does not mean you aren't doing a great deal of it already. It simply means that your own data use will include revisiting the key findings of the data and reviewing the decisions based on them as a *school*, so you can zero in on the priority targets for your own *personal* leadership work. You may have become aware of issues that you need to learn more about yourself before you can decide whether and how to include them in shared discussions and decision making. For example, you may have developed increased sensitivity about equity and cultural competence that you need to explore yourself and seek advice about how to surface and address with the school as a whole.

The second reassurance is that the "plus more" is within your control. It's setting your own agenda based on the questions, What do these data seem to tell me? What do they not tell me that I need to know? What data do we not have that we most need to have that I should pursue? and What constraints have I felt as I murmured, "But the district . . ."? These reflections will help you focus your professional goals and action steps—which you will also document—thereby generating even more data.

After all those "mores," take a deep breath and absorb this third reassurance: "plus more" is followed by "and less." Your sources of data and the findings (and wonderings) from them will initially expand so that you have a good look at all the things you *could* spend time on in order to make the best possible decisions about what you *can* and *will* spend time on. Your goals and action steps for your own performance must be a short list because it is humanly impossible to tackle everything that might need attention. Even if it *were* humanly possible for you as principal, it would probably not be possible for your staff to absorb all of it, and the overload could lead to fragmentation and fracturing of relationships.

Since this chapter ends by asking you to be transparent in your practice, I will model candor by sharing one of my own struggles. As a first-year principal, I became very discouraged because my days never ended with my to-do list complete. I called the veteran principal who had urged me to apply, brought me to the attention of a large central office administration, and I'm sure, influenced the selection committee. I was almost angry as I reminded him that he "got me into this," and then I began to apologize because I wasn't up to the job and he was going to be disappointed in me and embarrassed for recommending me. After listening patiently, he kindly asked, "What criteria are you using to decide if you are 'up to it' or not?"

I explained about all the things that needed my attention, and my long to-do lists, and the daily frustration of getting a few things done but going home at the end of the day with very few check marks and many more arrows moving the same tasks forward to the next day or week.

"You are using the wrong criteria to judge yourself. Tell me about the things you *did* accomplish and why you did them first," he said.

We talked more about the same realities you now face every day with interruptions and unanticipated events. The guidance he then imparted became a coping strategy in every subsequent position. He summarized it this way: "The *good* leader will always see more that needs doing than can be done. The *wise* leader is the one who makes the best decisions about what to leave *un*done for now. When you make your lists, put stars by only three things that will be your priorities for the day. If you accomplish only those, and you have made the right decisions about which ones they are, you will have been effective."

This chapter is about using data to help you make wise decisions about where to focus your efforts and which specific steps only you can take. You will end up with goals and action steps to advance your leadership and your school's data use.

How Will You Find the Data?

You have the data you need from all the sources used in your schoolwide planning. Your student-learning data are paramount, but your own leadership planning will also be influenced by perceptual data gathered formally or informally about the concerns of students, staff, and family and community constituents. As you developed your school improvement plan, you identified data that you will acquire and use as you and your school improvement/leadership team and data team monitor implementation and document the results of schoolwide decisions.

You have been gathering additional data through the process of reflection and journaling as you utilized "Your Role as Principal" at the end of each chapter. By the end of chapter 1, you had data in the form of comparing data uses in your school with recommended practices. After chapter 2, you had insights about the culture and structures in your school and may have identified sources of data you want to add to your use. You may also have examined your own assessment literacy confidence and identified some professional learning you want to pursue. The school improvement focus of chapter 3 included decisions about how to gather evidence of implementation and most certainly identified some tasks for you in that process. You may find it helpful to return to the reproducible Components of Data Use (page 46), and think about it now in terms of setting goals for your own work. Based on chapters 4 and 5, you may have begun to set priorities for your instructional leadership in supporting struggling learners and their teachers.

The reproducible Progress With Data Use chart (page 93) is an additional tool for assessing your role as principal in leading the use of data in your school. As you read across each row, put an X in the cell that most accurately describes your present reality. Then draw a line connecting the Xs to create a profile of your role as a data-using principal. These data will inform your planning and performance in the weeks ahead.

How Will You Use the Data?

Just as the first component of schoolwide use of data was *assembling the data*, you have gathered data specifically relative to your role as a data-friendly principal. The Progress With Data Use chart assisted you in *analyzing the current status* and *assessing current efforts* around data use in your school and in your own practice. You will also use the data in parallel ways for your planning, for improving your own performance (determining your next steps and ensuring implementation by setting procedures in place to document your progress), and for reporting your results.

The reproducible Modeling Use of Data to Propel Progress and Document Results (page 94) invites you to use the data you've collected and select the leadership actions you intend to take in the areas you have identified as priorities. This does *not* mean filling in all the rows and columns; rather, it means thinking strategically about where the leverage of your direct leadership is most needed and can have the most direct impact and a spin-off effect on other areas.

For example, the principal in chapter 5 who engaged staff around five elements of powerful teaching might have used the Strengthening Classroom Instruction part of this form, as shown in figure 6.1 (page 90).

The example in figure 6.2 (page 90) reflects the efforts of another principal who was concerned about survey results that were low in the area of administration-staff relationships. Openly sharing his concern in one-on-one conversations with a few of the most involved teacher leaders, he discovered that some staff members felt he didn't care about them or value their work because they never saw him or heard from him individually. Figure 6.2 includes the actions he chose, his approach to data gathering, and the results he achieved.

My Leadership Actions Related to:	How I Will Document My Progress	Statement of Results
Strengthening Classroom Instruction Gain staff agreement on short list of powerful instructional strategies as focus. Post in all rooms. Create walkthrough form based on them. Dedicate 1 to 1 1/2 hours per day, 3 days per week in calendar; inform secretary to hold. Report frequency of observed strategies at each staff meeting.	Log progress and decision about the list of strategies. Log date posters provided. Use walkthrough form to gather dates, classroom numbers visited, and checkmarks for any evidence of the strategy. Analyze data weekly. Create line graph for each strategy; update weekly. Post updated graphs at each faculty meeting. Use the walkthrough forms to tap a teacher to give an example at each meeting.	Goal was 30 walkthroughs per week; obtained average of 24.5. High expectations increased from 51% to 74%. Evidence of standards increased from 65% to 93%. Active student participation increased from 42% to 67%. Challenging material and higher-level questions increased from 39% to 63%. Frequent assessment and feedback increased slightly but only to 37%. Percent of students proficient or above in reading increased from 55% to 69%. Percent of students proficient or above in math increased from 42% to 62%.

Figure 6.1: Examples of strengthening classroom instruction from principals.

My Leadership Actions Related to:	How I Will Document My Progress	Statement of Results
Refining My Own Performance Interact with all staff frequently and equally. Provide more positive feedback. Ask for their needs and ideas.	Put staff list on my PDA. Add date of direct contact and code with + if gave positive feedback and ? if asked needs and ideas. Write positive note in PDA or jot down needs/ideas and save to email and file later.	First two weeks showed pattern of people missed, mostly in far wing and portables. Created a map for each day of week to rotate start point and to get to all areas. Survey sections on principal and staff relationships increased to average of 4.1 (from 3.2) on 5-point scale. Received 13 notes of appreciation for "noticing me," "valuing my work," and so on.

Figure 6.2: Examples of refining performance from principals.

Using these examples as a guide, make a copy of the reproducible on page 94. Review your data and select two to three areas for your own work. Identify your leadership actions and how will you document your progress. Anticipate several months from now when you will share your progress with your staff and your supervisor. One of the most powerful ways you will use data is to be transparent about your own practice—modeling your goal-setting, sharing your struggles to learn, doing new things, creating a different balance in your use of time and resources, and celebrating the results.

Your Role as Principal

Data-Based Decision Making—what fun! Yes, it does sound more like going to the dentist than to the Fourth of July picnic. But when the data shed light on a perplexing problem, it can be the dawning of a new day—and when data reveal results to celebrate, it is truly fireworks. Take the work seriously but hold it lightly and maintain a sense of humor.

One day as I struggled to unravel some knotty data, my mind strayed to a bit of Shakespeare and began to play. The result was a parody on Hamlet's famous soliloquy, raising the decision for you "to data, or not to data." I hope this last offering may amuse and inspire you when you face dilemmas on your data journey.

> To data, or not to data—
>
> > That is the question.
>
> Whether 'tis nobler in the mind to suffer
>
> > The ambiguity of lack of feedback,
>
> Or take up the risk of setting goals—
>
> > And by setting goals, thus be accountable for evidence.
>
>
> To try—to risk . . .
>
> And more—by goals to say we can improve
>
> > And will excel, despite the heartache
> >
> > And the thousand natural shocks that flesh is heir to.
>
>
> To try—to risk . . .
>
> To risk, perchance to fail; ay, there's the rub;
>
> But 'tis only in the risk the dreams may come.
>
> That dreams may come to weary staff,
>
> And thus to kindle dreams in students' hearts—

There's the respect!

There's the joy!

This makes the legacy of hard-worked life.

For who would wish to be relaxed,

Complacent in our current mode

When patient merit more worthy makes

 And the hope of something better yet

 Makes us rather bear those goals

Than never see yon evidence of implementation

and impact on the learning minds.

Thus, data makes thinkers of us all—

And thrusts us forward

 Into enterprises of great pitch and moment—

Haste we now!

For learning is the quest

We share in equal part—

 With peers and pupils, aye,

Take heart! Take heart! Take heart!

Progress With Data Use

Needs Attention	Progressing	Skillful
Use of data is considered the principal's job.	Use of data is considered the responsibility of a designated group or team.	All staff engage in periodic, scheduled data discussions.
Principal relies on district staff to interpret data.	Principal has developed basic assessment literacy.	Principal leads data discussions and models both understanding of the data and inquiry about them.
Principal distributes test results to tested grades only.	Principal forms vertical data team and is actively involved in data analysis.	Principal models use of data with frequent references and questions.
Principal urges teachers to work together.	Principal honors district directives about use of time for collaboration.	Principal redirects time to ensure data-enhanced teacher collaboration.
Principal leads data use focused on annual state test results.	Data use includes state and district assessments and other state-required data (for example, attendance, suspensions).	Data use includes multiple measures of student learning, plus objective and subjective data regarding students, staff, and family and community factors.
Principal assumes that initial training ensures implementation.	Principal and staff agree on indicators of implementation and methods of gathering evidence.	Evidence of implementation is gathered frequently, shared with all staff, and used to adjust professional development.
Teachers give textbook-related tests, record grades, and move on.	Teachers develop or select and give formative assessments based on most essential concepts and skills.	Results of formative assessments are used weekly for instructional planning and to plan interventions.
Principal completes formal evaluations as required.	Principal completes formal evaluation cycles and makes frequent informal classroom visits.	Principal engages staff in discussions of evidence of student learning.
Principal meets district directives for use of data.	Principal sets goals for leadership that match schoolwide goals for student learning.	Principal is transparent and models use of data to set goals and document professional growth.

Modeling Use of Data to Propel Progress and Document Results

My Leadership Actions Related to:	How I Will Document My Progress	Statement of Results
Cultivating the Culture		
Clarifying Structures and Processes		
Ensuring Implementation of Schoolwide Strategies From the School Improvement Plan		
Designing Support for Struggling Students		
Strengthening Classroom Instruction		
Refining My Own Performance		

REFERENCES AND RESOURCES

Barr, R. D., & Parrett, W. H. (2007). *The kids left behind: Catching up the underachieving children of poverty.* Bloomington, IN: Solution Tree Press.

Boudett, K. P., & Moody, L. (2005). Organizing for collaborative work. In K. P. Boudett, E. A. City, & R. J. Murnane (Eds.), *Data wise: A step-by-step guide to using assessment results to improve teaching and learning* (pp. 11–28). Cambridge, MA: Harvard Education Press.

Boudett, K. P., & Steele, J. L. (Eds.). (2007). *Data wise in action: Stories of schools using data to improve teaching and learning.* Cambridge, MA: Harvard Education Press.

Brown-Chidsey, R. (2007). No more "waiting to fail": How response to intervention works and why it is needed. *Educational Leadership, 65*(2), 40–46.

Bryk, A., & Schneider, B. (2002). *Trust in schools.* New York: Russell Sage.

Canter, A., Klotz, M. B., & Cowan, K. (2008). Response to intervention: The future for secondary schools. *Principal Leadership, 8*(6), 12–15.

Center for Comprehensive School Reform and Improvement. (2006). *Program evaluation for the practitioner: Using evaluation as a school improvement strategy.* Washington, DC: Author.

City, E. A., Kagle, M., & Teoh, M. B. (2005). Examining instruction. In K. P. Boudett, E. A. City, & R. J. Murnane (Eds.), *Data wise: A step-by-step guide to using assessment results to improve teaching and learning* (pp. 97–115). Cambridge, MA: Harvard Education Press.

Connecticut State Department of Education. (2000). *Connecticut's blueprint for reading achievement: The report of the Early Reading Success Panel.* Hartford, CT: Author. Accessed at www.state.ct.us/sde/dtl/curriculum/currcbra.htm on July 21, 2011.

Creighton, T. B. (2007). *Schools and data: The educator's guide for using data to improve decision making* (2nd ed.). Thousand Oaks, CA: Corwin Press.

Cromey, A., & Hanson, M. (2000). *An exploratory analysis of school-based student assessment systems.* Oak Brook, IL: North Central Regional Educational Laboratory. Accessed at www.ncrel.org/policy/pubs/html/data/ on July 21, 2011.

Depka, E. (2006). *The data guidebook for teachers and leaders: Tools for continuous improvement.* Thousand Oaks, CA: Corwin Press.

DuFour, R., DuFour, R., Eaker, R., & Karhanek, G. (2010). *Raising the bar and closing the gap: Whatever it takes.* Bloomington, IN: Solution Tree Press.

Earl, L., & Katz, S. (2006). *Leading schools in a data-rich world: Harnessing data for school improvement.* Thousand Oaks, CA: Corwin Press.

Fullan, M. (2003, January). *Leading in a culture of change.* Handout provided at the meeting of the Office of Superintendent of Public Instruction, Spokane, WA.

Fullan, M. (2005). *Leadership and sustainability: System thinkers in action.* Thousand Oaks, CA: Corwin Press.

Fullan, M. (2009). Have theory, will travel: A theory of action for system change. In A. Hargreaves & M. Fullan (Eds.), *Change wars* (pp. 275–293). Bloomington, IN: Solution Tree Press.

Gregory, G. H., & Kuzmich, L. (2004). *Data driven differentiation in the standards-based classroom.* Thousand Oaks, CA: Corwin Press.

Gregory, G. H., & Kuzmich, L. (2007). *Teacher teams that get results: 61 strategies for sustaining and renewing professional learning communities.* Thousand Oaks, CA: Corwin Press.

Guskey, T. R. (2007). Using assessments to improve teaching and learning. In D. Reeves (Ed.), *Ahead of the curve: The power of assessment to transform teaching and learning* (pp. 15–29). Bloomington, IN: Solution Tree Press.

Hall, S. (2008). *A principal's guide to implementing response to intervention.* Thousand Oaks, CA: Corwin Press.

Hargreaves, A. (2009). The fourth way of change: Towards an age of inspiration and sustainability. In A. Hargreaves & M. Fullan (Eds.), *Change wars* (pp. 11–43). Bloomington, IN: Solution Tree Press.

Heritage, M., & Yeagerly, R. (2005). Data use and school improvement: Challenges and prospects. In J. L. Herman & E. H. Haertel (Eds.), *Uses and misuses of data for educational accountability and improvement.* Malden, MA: Blackwell.

Hirsh, S. (2009). Foreword. In J. Killion & P. Roy, *Becoming a learning school.* Oxford, OH: National Staff Development Council.

Hirsh, S. (2011). Teacher evaluation: An opportunity to leverage learning at all levels. *The Learning System, 6*(1), 1, 4–5.

Holcomb, E. (2004). *Getting excited about data* (2nd ed.). Thousand Oaks, CA: Corwin Press.

Holcomb, E. (2007). *Students are stakeholders too! Including every voice in authentic high school reform.* Thousand Oaks, CA: Corwin Press.

Holcomb, E. L. (2009). *Asking the right questions: Tools for collaboration and school change* (3rd ed.). Thousand Oaks, CA: Corwin Press.

Holcomb, E. L. (2010). Customer input through focus groups. *PAGE ONE, 32*(1), 22–25.

Holcomb, E. L. (2012). *Data dynamics: Aligning teacher team, school, and district efforts.* Bloomington, IN: Solution Tree Press.

Holland, P. (2005). The case for expanding standards for teacher evaluation to include an instructional supervision perspective. *Journal of Personnel Evaluation in Education, 18,* 67–77.

Hord, S. M. (2003). *Learning together, leading together: Changing schools through professional learning communities.* New York: Teachers College Press.

Hord, S. M., & Sommers, W. A. (2008). *Leading professional learning communities: Voices from research and practice.* Thousand Oaks, CA: Corwin Press.

Horowitz, S. H. (2005). *Response to intervention: A primer—The facts about LD classification.* Accessed at www.ncld.org/at-school/general-topics/parentschool-partnership/response-to-intervention-a-primer on July 21, 2011.

Johnson, E., Mellard, D. F., Fuchs, D., & McKnight, M. A. (2006). *Responsiveness to intervention (RTI): How to do it.* Lawrence, KS: National Research Center on Learning Disabilities. Accessed at http://nrcld.org/rti_manual/ on July 21, 2011.

Johnston, J., Knight, M., & Miller, L. (2007). Finding time for teams. *Journal of Staff Development, 28*(2), 14–18.

Kaplan, L. S., & Owings, W. A. (2001). Teacher quality and student achievement: Recommendations for principals. *NASSP Bulletin, 85*(628), 64–73. Accessed at www.principals.org/news/bltn_tch_qul_stdnt_ach1101.htm.

Killion, J., & Bellamy, G. T. (2000). On the job: Data analysts focus school improvement efforts. *Journal of Staff Development, 21*(1). Accessed at www.learningforward.org/news/jsd/killion211.cfm on July 21, 2011.

Knapp, M. S., Swinnerton, J. A., Copland, M. A., & Monpas-Huber, J. (2006). *Data-informed leadership in education: A research report in collaboration with the Wallace Foundation.* Seattle: Center for the Study of Teaching and Policy, University of Washington. Accessed at http://depts.washington.edu/ctpmail/PDFs/DataInformed-Nov1.pdf on July 21, 2011.

Lambert, L. (2003). *Leadership capacity for lasting school improvement.* Alexandria, VA: Association for Supervision and Curriculum Development.

Langer, G. M., Colton, A. B., & Goff, L. (2003). *Collaborative analysis of student work: Improving teaching and learning.* Alexandria, VA: Association for Supervision and Curriculum Development.

Louis, K. S., Leithwood, K., Wahlstrom, K., & Anderson, S. E. (2010). *Learning from leadership: Investigating the links to improved student learning.* St. Paul: University of Minnesota.

Marshall, K. (2003). Recovering from HSPS (hyperactive superficial principal syndrome): A progress report. *Phi Delta Kappan, 84*(9), 701–709.

Marshall, K. (2006a). *Interim assessments: Keys to successful implementation.* New York: New Leaders for New Schools. Accessed at www.marshallmemo.com/articles/Interim%20Assmt%20Report%20Apr.%2012,%2006.pdf on July 21, 2011.

Marshall, K. (2006b). Teacher evaluation rubrics: The why and the how. *EDge Magazine.* Accessed at www.marshallmemo.com/articles/EDge%20Rubrics%20Jan.%2025,%2006.doc on July 21, 2011.

Marzano, R. J. (2007). *The art and science of teaching: A comprehensive framework for effective instruction.* Alexandria, VA: Association for Supervision and Curriculum Development.

Marzano, R. J. (2010). *Formative assessment & standards-based grading.* Bloomington, IN: Marzano Research Laboratory.

McEnery, D. (2005). Getting out of the way: A lesson in change. *Principal Leadership, 5*(9), 42–46.

Mellard, D. E, & Johnson, E. (2008). *RTI: A practitioner's guide to implementing response to intervention.* Thousand Oaks, CA: Corwin Press.

Meyers, E., & Rust, F. O. (2000). The test doesn't tell all: How teachers know that their students are learning. *Education Week, 19*(38), 34, 37.

National Association of Elementary School Principals. (2001). *Leading learning communities: Standards for what principals should know and be able to do.* Alexandria, VA: Author.

National Association of Elementary School Principals. (2008). *Leading learning communities: Standards for what principals should know and be able to do* (2nd ed.). Alexandria, VA: Author.

National Center for Learning Disabilities. (n.d.). Core findings about response to intervention. *LD InfoZone.* Accessed at www.ncld.org/content/view/1220/389/.

O'Connor, K. (2007). The last frontier: Tackling the grading dilemma. In D. Reeves (Ed.), *Ahead of the curve: The power of assessment to transform teaching and learning* (pp. 127–145). Bloomington, IN: Solution Tree Press.

Olson, L. (2007). Instant read on reading, in palms of their hands. *Education Week, 26*(35), 24–34. Accessed at www.edweek.org/ew/articles/2007/05/02/35form-nm.h26.html?qs=instant%20read on July 21, 2011.

O'Neill, J., & Conzemius, A. (2006). *The power of SMART goals: Using goals to improve student learning.* Bloomington, IN: Solution Tree Press.

Philadelphia Education Fund. (n.d.). *Guidelines for looking at student work.* Accessed at www.philaedfund.org/slcweb/guideli.htm.

Reeves, D. B. (2004). *Accountability in learning: How teachers and school leaders can take charge.* Alexandria, VA: Association for Supervision and Curriculum Development.

Reeves, D. B. (2006). *The learning leader: How to focus school improvement for better results.* Alexandria, VA: Association for Supervision and Curriculum Development.

Reeves, D. B. (2007). Challenges and choices: The role of educational leaders in effective assessment. In D. Reeves (Ed.), *Ahead of the curve: The power of assessment to transform teaching and learning* (pp. 227–251). Bloomington, IN: Solution Tree Press.

Sawchuk, S. (2011). Wanted: Ways to assess the majority of teachers. *Education Week, 30*(19), 1. Accessed at www.edweek.org/ew/articles/2011/02/02/19teachers_ep.h30.html on July 21, 2011.

Schilling, S. G., Carlisle, J. F., Scott, S. E., & Zeng, J. (2007). Are fluency measures accurate predictors of reading achievement? *Elementary School Journal, 107*(5), 429–448.

Schmoker, M. (2010, September 29). When pedagogic fads trump priorities. *Education Week.* Accessed at www.edweek.org/ew/articles/2010/09/29/05.schmoker.h30.html on July 21, 2011.

Shirley, D. (2009). The music of democracy: Emerging strategies for a new era of post-standardization. In A. Hargreaves & M. Fullan (Eds.), *Change wars* (pp. 135–160). Bloomington, IN: Solution Tree Press.

Stansbury, K. (2001). The role of formative assessment in induction programs. *New Teacher Center Reflections, 4*(2), 1–2.

Stiggins, R. J. (2007). Assessment through the student's eyes. *Educational Leadership, 64*(8), 22–26.

Stiggins, R. J., Arter, J. A., Chappuis, J., & Chappuis, S. (2004). *Classroom assessment* for *student learning: Doing it right—Using it well*. Portland, OR: Assessment Training Institute.

Texas Reading First. (2007). Progress monitoring: An essential step in the assessment cycle. *Texas Reading First Quarterly, 1*(4), 2, 4.

Wade, H. H. (2001). *Data inquiry and analysis for educational reform* (ERIC Digest No. 153). Eugene, OR: ERIC Clearinghouse on Educational Management. Accessed at https://scholarsbank.uoregon.edu/dspace/bitstream/1794/3376/1/digest153.pdf on July 21, 2011.

Walser, N. (2007). Response to intervention. *Harvard Education Letter, 23*(1). Accessed at www.hepg.org/hel/article/239 on July 21, 2011.

Williams, M., Cray, M., Millen, E., & Protheroe, N. (2002). *Essentials for principals: Effective teacher observations*. Alexandria, VA: National Association of Elementary School Principals.

INDEX

A

Anderson, S. E., 7

Arter, J. A., 42

assessment(s)

    benchmark (interim), 43

    classroom instruction and diagnostic, 57–58

    cloze, 51

    formative, 43, 50

    frameworks, 49–50, 66

    literacy, 11, 18, 50–52

    math, 52

    need for multiple forms of, 53–54

    process-oriented, 51

    reading, 51–52

    student self-assessment, 56–57

    summative, 43

    testing versus, 50

B

beliefs versus behaviors, changed, 27

Bellamy, G. T., 29

benchmark (interim) assessments, 43

Black, P., 43–44

Boudett, K. P., 17–18, 26, 27

C

Brown-Chidsey, R., 59, 60, 62–63

Bryk, A., 27

Carlisle, J. F., 51

Center for American Progress, 68

Center for Comprehensive School Reform and Improvement, 11

Chappuis, J., 42

Chappuis, S., 42

Citizens' Commission on Civil Rights, 5

City, E. A., 25

classroom instruction, data to support

    collaborative analysis of student work, 76–80

    conversations with teachers, 80

    data, finding, 73–80

    data, how to use, 80–83

    data, identifying, 70–72

    diagnostic assessment, 57–58

    feedback, 81–82

    goals protocol, 78–79

    implementation, evidence of, 71

    instructional strategies, evidence of, 71

    peer observation, 75

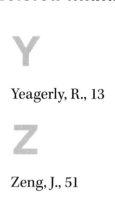

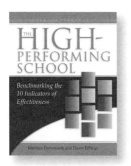

The High-Performing School: Benchmarking the 10 Indicators of Effectiveness
Mardale Dunsworth and Dawn Billings
Learn the improvement process used by many schools to become high-performing schools. This book is a guide to the on-site school review—a cooperative venture between an external review team and a school's administrators, teachers, and students. **BKF294**

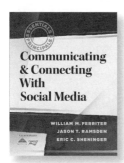

Communicating and Connecting With Social Media
William M. Ferriter, Jason T. Ramsden, and Eric C. Sheninger
Social media holds great potential benefits for schools reaching out to our communities, preparing our teachers, and connecting with our kids. In this short text, the authors examine how enterprising schools are using social media tools to provide customized professional development for teachers and to transform communication practices with staff, students, parents, and other stakeholders. **BKF474**

The School Leader's Guide to Professional Learning Communities at Work™
Richard DuFour and Rebecca DuFour
Are you a K–8 principal looking to implement the PLC at Work™ process? Explore the components needed to lay the foundation, including how to develop a structure that supports collaborative teams, how to focus on effective monitoring strategies, and more. **BKF489**

Collaborative Teams in Professional Learning Communities at Work™
Learning by Doing
Richard DuFour, Rebecca DuFour, Robert Eaker, and Thomas Many
This short program shows exactly what collaborative teams do. Aligned with the best-selling book Learning by Doing, the video features unscripted footage of collaboration in action. Learn how teams organize, interact, and find time to meet; what products they produce; and more. **DVF023**

Data Dynamics
Aligning Teacher Team, School, & District Efforts
By Edie L. Holcomb
Examine the ways your school can better use student achievement data, nonacademic student data, staff data, and parent/community data to identify areas for improvement. Designed to help administrators and leaders, this book also details how teachers can use good data to monitor and motivate students. **BKF424**

Solution Tree | Press
a division of
Solution Tree
Visit solution-tree.com or call 800.733.6786 to order.

Solution Tree

Solution Tree's mission is to advance the work of our authors. By working with the best researchers and educators worldwide, we strive to be the premier provider of innovative publishing, in-demand events, and inspired professional development designed to transform education to ensure that all students learn.

The mission of the National Association of Elementary School Principals is to lead in the advocacy and support for elementary and middle level principals and other education leaders in their commitment for all children.